Mana Whakatipu

Ngāi Tahu leader Mark Solomon on leadership and life

Mark Solomon
with Mark Revington

MASSEY UNIVERSITY PRESS

Contents

Mō tātou, ā, mō kā
uri ā muri ake nei.

For us and our
children after us.

Foreword

This is the memoir of Tā Mark Solomon, as told by him. It is also intended to give a reader some insight into what makes Tā Mark such an effective leader — but let's just say his actions often speak louder than his words.

He is known as a respected Māori leader, a forthright man, intelligent, unafraid to speak his mind, with a strong sense of justice. He is a man whom people will happily follow. Tā Mark has said himself: 'If people are doing things that I think are incorrect, I will stand up and challenge them.'

Tā Mark has an extraordinary backstory, from foundry worker to leader of one of the largest and wealthiest iwi in New Zealand. He is a man with a good deal of influence on a national level.

Dame Naida Glavish, of Ngāti Whātua, describes him as a brilliant leader and speaker. 'He also cares enough to address the issues that others wouldn't dare address,' she says. 'For instance, Mark would speak strongly about domestic violence, whether that domestic violence is right under his nose or under someone else's.'

A brief outline of his life follows. Tā Mark, who was born in Ōtautahi Christchurch in 1954, married Maria (née Howie) in 1974. It was, he reckons, a case of love at first sight. They raised four children and have a whāngai or adopted son. The children don't feature in this book as Tā Mark agreed to tell his story as long as he didn't talk about his family.

He grew up in Ōtautahi but the family spent as much time as possible at Ōaro, a small coastal settlement 20 kilometres south of Kaikōura, where his father's parents had land. The death of his father, George, when Mark was only 12 had a major impact on his early life. George was only 39.

Mark spent the first part of his professional life as a foundryman, having previously worked in Ōtautahi in a freezing works, on a shearing gang, and as a pāua diver. It's hard to know what would have happened had he continued as a foundryman, but in 1995 he was elected to Te Rūnanga o Ngāi Tahu, the tribal council of Ngāi Tahu, as the representative for Kaikōura. It would change his life.

Ngāi Tahu, the most commercially astute iwi in Aotearoa and the largest tribe of Te Waipounamu, has 18 representatives on its council, each elected by the iwi's 18 papatipu rūnanga or regional councils.

In 1995, Ngāi Tahu was about to settle its Waitangi Tribunal claim with the Crown, ending seven generations of pursuit of justice after the Crown had reneged on land deals made by Ngāi Tahu leaders and left the iwi impoverished. Three years later, in 1998, as the tribe embarked on a new future, Tā Mark was elected kaiwhakahaere of the iwi, just days before the Ngāi Tahu Claims Settlement Act was to have its third and final reading in Parliament. It was the second major Waitangi Tribunal claim, behind Waikato Tainui, to be settled. Tā Mark was kaiwhakahaere of Ngāi Tahu for 18 years, until 2016.

In 2005, he was instrumental in establishing the Iwi Chairs Forum, a group representing iwi from across New Zealand. The forum, which meets four times a year, was fired by Tā Mark's belief that, together, Māori are unstoppable. As he saw it, every tribe in the country was trying to do the same thing. They were all trying to build a capital base, to look after the social and cultural needs of their people and to protect their respective areas. What he didn't understand was, if they were all doing the same thing, why were they doing it in isolation? The forum held its first meeting at Takahanga Marae in Kaikōura, which Tā Mark's uncle, Bill Solomon, helped build.

Tā Mark was a board member of the Museum of New Zealand Te Papa Tongarewa from 2002 to 2007 and an original member of the Minister of Māori Affairs' Māori Economic Taskforce, established in 2009. At that time, the Minister of Māori Affairs was Dr Pita Sharples and the taskforce had a budget of $4.5 million per annum to research and implement Māori economic development initiatives.

In 2011, he played a key role in setting up the Māori trades training initiative, He Toki ki te Rika, funded by Ngāi Tahu, and he is the founding patron of He Toki. In 2012, he was named a Visionary Leader at the Deloitte and *New Zealand Management* magazine national business awards.

He became Tā Mark, or Sir Mark, in 2013, when he was made a Knight Companion of the New Zealand Order of Merit for services to Māori and business. In 2015, he received an honorary doctorate from Lincoln University, as Doctor of Natural Resources, and he was also appointed to the National Science Challenges governance boards for the Sustainable Seas and Deep South projects.

In 2016, he announced his resignation as the representative of Kaikōura on the Ngāi Tahu table and as kaiwhakahaere of Te Rūnanga o Ngāi Tahu. The same year, he was awarded a Kea World Class New Zealand Award. Since stepping down as kaiwhakahaere, he has been deputy chair and then acting chair of the Canterbury District Health Board. He chairs Te Pūtahitanga o Te Waipounamu (the Whānau Ora commissioning agency for Te Waipounamu, which was set up by the nine iwi in the south), and he chairs the Māori Carbon Foundation, an organisation that plants trees on marginal land and trades in carbon credits.

He is a champion for Tū Pono: Te Mana Kaha o te Whānau, a pilot programme launched in 2017 by Te Pūtahitanga o Te Waipounamu to explore ways of enabling stronger Māori responses to family harm and violence; he was a key driver in the establishment of, and is a signatory to, the Children's Covenant, written by Judge Carolyn Henwood and launched in

2016. The Covenant commits to protecting children from violence, abuse, neglect and to provide a proper standard of living. It also promises to support their emotional and mental well-being, provide education and take children's views into account.

Tā Mark has been approached by all this country's main political parties but has resisted a career in national politics. He is constantly in demand as a speaker, and has been co-opted onto a number of government committees. He is usually reluctant to talk about himself. But he has an innate grasp of leadership — mana whakatipu — in a way that is extremely powerful. He believes that leaders must stride confidently between multiple cultures and be as comfortable on the global corporate stage as they are on the marae.

He is known for his mana, honesty, integrity and effective leadership. This book gives insights into how he has applied these throughout his life.

Mark Revington
May 2021

Big day out

In the beginning, I was tongue-tied and terrified. I had been a member of the Ngāi Tahu council — what we call 'the table' — for three years, but here I was, in September 1998, newly elected as kaiwhakahaere or chair of Te Rūnanga o Ngāi Tahu and I had to front up on one of our biggest days in 150 years: the third and final reading in Parliament of the Ngāi Tahu Claims Settlement Bill.

This settlement has been hailed as one of the pioneering negotiations of the modern Treaty of Waitangi settlement process and set precedents for all negotiations that have followed. For Ngāi Tahu, who occupy the major part of Te Waipounamu, the South Island, it was seen as some level of justice and redress for the wrongs that had been committed against us, even if it was too little and too late. In the nineteenth century, our ancestors, who had long had contact with Europeans and intermarried with them, had sold land to the Crown — 80 per cent of Te Waipounamu, in fact — but the Crown had not honoured the deal. Ngāi Tahu was ripped off. The tribe had been fighting to overturn that wrong for seven generations.

The Crown reckoned full redress was worth around $12 to $15 billion. Our advisers thought it was closer to $20 billion. We settled for $170 million — a lot less, but it allowed Ngāi Tahu to move forward, to rebuild. And that we would: by the time I stepped down as kaiwhakahaere 18 years later, Ngāi Tahu had assets worth more than $1.5 billion and the tribe was widely regarded as economically astute.

Outside the Grand Hall of Parliament, there were television crews and more than a hundred people waiting to be welcomed. As Ngāi Tahu kaiwhakahaere, it was my job to deliver the whaikōrero on behalf of Ngāi Tahu, but my grasp of te reo Māori was basic at best. I'd never been a public person and I was terrified.

I stammered through the pōwhiri, and afterwards

I realised that I hadn't acknowledged all the rangatira from other tribes who had come to tautoko us, support us. I was hugely embarrassed.

When I went to explain, I found them all standing together.

'Uncle,' I said to Api Mahuika, the leader of Ngāti Porou. 'I've come to apologise for not acknowledging you being here to support Ngāi Tahu.'

Api looked at me with a big smile on his face and said, 'Oh, boy. We could see the tūtae running down the back of your legs.'

He had forgiven me. That afternoon, I began to realise the goodwill that existed in the highest echelons of the government towards Ngāi Tahu. At the pōwhiri, we did the hongi and the harirū, then shook hands. When I got up to Jim Bolger, who, after a leadership challenge, had left Parliament four months earlier, he had his business card in his hand. He slipped it into mine and said, 'My private number's on there. Any support or help you need, ring whenever you like.' It was the first time I had met him. The same thing happened with Doug Graham, who was then the Minister of Treaty Negotiations.

It had taken seven years to reach settlement, since the Waitangi Tribunal hearings in which Ngāi Tahu had conclusively proved that we had been rorted by the Crown, but now Bolger and Graham were more than happy to help.

Two months later, Bolger's successor as prime minister, Jenny Shipley, delivered the Crown's apology to Ngāi Tahu at Ōnuku Marae, near Akaroa on Banks Peninsula.

We are a people of long memory. Some of our whakataukī appear in this book. Our ancestors had signed the Treaty in 1840 at Ōnuku, Ōtakou and Ruapuke Island. Finally we were getting some justice. Many Ngāi Tahu had fought for this moment.

Whakapapa

I can trace my whakapapa back 22 generations to Tahupōtiki, the founding tipuna of Ngāi Tahu — the iwi in fact takes its name from him. Tahupōtiki was a descendant of Paikea and a close relative of Porourangi, Ngāti Porou's ancestor.

Many generations ago, the descendants of Tahupōtiki, who was originally from the East Coast of the North Island, moved south and eventually established mana whenua, or territorial rights, in Te Waipounamu by integrating with Ngāti Māmoe and Waitaha iwi.

This process of Ngāi Tahu melding with these earlier communities was still occurring when Europeans arrived on the islands in the eighteenth century.

Coming closer to my generation, on my father's side, that whakapapa is a bit like a League of Nations. The first Solomon in New Zealand was an American Jew by the name of Abraham Solomon. Actually, his name was Abraham Solomon-Score but he shortened it. He was a whaler who set sail from Nantucket in 1856. He married a Banks Peninsula Ngāi Tahu woman called Toko. Their firstborn was Tieki, who married Ripeka Paraone. She was the daughter of Pikimauka and had been married before. Abraham and Toko had seven daughters and one son, Aperahama, who was the father of my grandfather, Rangi Solomon.

My grandfather's mum was Amelia Henrici. She was German and Ngāti Kahungunu from Ngāti Pāhauwera of Mohaka on the East Coast of the North Island, near Wairoa. In fact, when the Hauhau attacked the Ngāti Pāhauwera pā in 1869, her older sister, who married a Hokianga from Akaroa, scaled a cliff to escape from the pā and carried my grandfather's mother, who was then a baby, down in her arms.

That sister brought up my grandfather's mother. My dad's mum was French-Māori. The French comes from a man called Jean Beaton-Morel, who came to Wairoa in the 1850s and married a Kahungunu woman from Wairoa named Irihapeti Kino. The Morels are pretty well known up in that region as fundraisers and builders of Catholic churches.

They had a son, Hoani Pitiroa Papeta Beaton-Morel, sometimes known as Teone Morēra, who came down to Little River for the marriage of his sister, Makareta, to a Robinson of the Robinson families of Little River. On that visit, he met a Wairewa woman by the name of Mereaina Pere and married her. Wairewa is one of the Ngāi Tahu papatipu rūnanga, or regional councils, and their marae is in the Ōkana valley on the eastern side of Te Roto o Wairewa (Lake Wairewa), past Little River on the road from Christchurch to Akaroa. The Māori transliteration of Beaton-Morel was Pītini-Morēra.

Their firstborn was John Beaton-Morel, who married my great-grandmother, Hariata Whakatau from Kaikōura. So, I've got German, French, Jewish and Māori from my father, and English and Danish from my mother.

The Māori is Waitaha, Ngāti Māmoe, Ngāi Tahu, Ngāti Kahungunu, Ngāti Pāhauwera and also Ngā Rauru, a south Taranaki iwi. Mereaina Pere was the daughter of a man called Hautapu Pere. His name appears in the Blue Book of Ngāi Tahu, the book published in 1925 and 1929 by the Ngāi Tahu Census Committees and which contains all the names of those Ngāi Tahu kaumātua alive in 1848 and 1853. It sets out our whakapapa.

One day, I was at work at what was then the Te Rūnanga o Ngāi Tahu head office in Hereford Street, Ōtautahi, when there was a knock on the door. I looked up. An old lady was standing in the doorway holding a sheet of paper. 'Here, dear,' she said. 'Here's your Ngā Rauru whakapapa.'

'Oh, tāua,' I replied. 'I think you've got me mixed up. I'm not Ngā Rauru.'

Tāua is Ngāi Tahu dialect. It actually means 'grandmother' but we use it as a mark of respect.

'Have a look at this list of names,' she said. 'Do you recognise anybody?'

I looked, and there was Mereaina.

I said, 'Oh, this is my great-great-grandmother.'

'Yes, dear. And all those others there are her brothers and sisters. In your Blue Book, you've got Hautapu Pere, but he's not Ngāi Tahu. He's tūturu Ngā Rauru, born in Waverley. This is your land reserve there. It's called Rangitatau. It's your family that's in it. But for some reason, the elders at Wairewa put him in the Ngāi Tahu Blue Book. When it went for a review, he was left in and we can't take him out. But Ngā Rauru is adamant that Hautapu Pere is not Ngāi Tahu. He's Ngā Rauru. But he married Meteria Te Ruru, who is Ngāi Tahu, from Little River. Of course, their daughter is also Mereaina.'

I have Waitaha connections, as do all Ngāi Tahu. I definitely have Ngāti Māmoe connections, as do all Ngāi Tahu. To explain: Ngāi Tahu is now a generic term for older tribes that have been incorporated within its authority. Those tribes include Waitaha and Ngāti Māmoe. It is widely accepted that Ngāti Māmoe came down from the East Coast of the North Island, Te Ika a Māui, and were followed a century later by Ngāi Tahu, who established ahi kā, customary right, through warfare and marriage.

I'm Ngāi Tahu, I'm Ngā Rauru and I'm Kahungunu from Wairoa and from Mohaka, which is Ngāti Pāhauwera. I've got land up there at Mohaka, next door to the old round whare. The proper name of my Uncle Martin — Uncle Dick, as we used to call him — was Matenga Te Auhia, who was his Ngāti Pāhauwera great-great-grandfather.

My dad's family was a huge influence on my life, although my dad didn't spend a lot of time on tribal politics, unlike my grandfather, Rangi. But Dad was well known and highly regarded among Māori. Once, when I went up to speak to Ngāi Tahu in Whangārei (when I was kaiwhakahaere we would speak to Ngāi Tahu groups all around Aotearoa), we were having dinner when an old Ngāpuhi man sitting opposite me said, 'I used to know a Solomon when I was in Christchurch. A man called George Solomon.'

'That was my dad,' I said.

'On the trams?'

'Yeah, that was my dad.'

'We Ngāpuhi will never forget your father,' he said. 'The first day your father started, he came into the smoko room in the Square, and he came and sat at the table with us. And these other Māori said, "Oh, don't sit with them, they're the killers of babies," which was what Ngāpuhi was always accused of. And your father just said, "Yeah, and I'm tangata whenua, and I'll sit wherever I like." None of us will forget your father. How is your dad?'

When I told him my father had died in 1966, the old man burst out crying.

My grandfather, Rangi Solomon, was a fisherman

who was born at Koukourārata, Port Levy, on Banks Peninsula. At one time, Koukourārata was the largest Māori settlement in Canterbury and was known as the food basket of the region.

I understand my grandfather skippered a ferry between Lyttelton and Koukourārata. He also was a flounderman. When he married my grandmother, they moved up to run the farm at Ōaro. Then, just after the Second World War, he started fishing and he stayed a fisherman until he died at sea in 1977.

He was on the Ngāi Tahu Māori Trust Board from the 1950s until he passed, and as kids we knew all about Ngāi Tahu because the tribe's affairs were always discussed.

I can remember going to Rāpaki with my grandfather when I was a teenager. Rāpaki, the small settlement near Lyttelton, was one of four Banks Peninsula, or Horomaka, Ngāi Tahu rūnanga based around marae. We walked into the old whare to see a whole back wall of young ladies. My grandfather had walked in first. He stopped dead and told us — me, my brother Wayne and our cousin Ned — to get back in the car.

'Grandad, don't be hasty. Look at them,' Wayne said.

‘Get in the car,’ he growled. They were all our cousins, and my grandfather was not impressed that we seemed keen on them. As we went out, I heard him say to someone, ‘I told you they’re too closely related. And you are not arranging their marriages.’

Funnily enough, he’d been the one who got me interested in tribal politics and whakapapa when he explained about Ngāi Tahu being a tribe of cousins. I’ve got 68,000 of them. It’s simply that some cousins are closer than others, and he was only too aware of the fact.

Mum

My mum's dad, Walter, was born in Uckfield, Sussex. He and his two brothers immigrated to New Zealand just before the First World War and opened a soft-drink factory in Dunedin called Hemsley Brothers Cordials.

Mum's maternal great-grandfather was a ship's mate called Alexander Edward Parks. He met a woman on the trip over from England, married her and became a lighthouse keeper at Godley Head, on the headland out from Lyttelton. They went from there to Akaroa, from there to the Nuggets in Otago, and from the Nuggets to Puysegur Point in the far southwest of Fiordland. Puysegur Point was described as remote, even for a lighthouse, and pummelled by frequent gale-force winds, heavy rain and sandflies. He was ill on that lighthouse for over a month before he got taken off.

We don't know what the illness was, but he was taken to Invercargill Hospital and died the morning they got him there. The moment he died, they made my mother's grandfather, Edward Morris Parks, a junior lighthouse keeper so that his mother and his siblings' children had a house to live in. I think there were 10 of them and he was just a teenager then. The whole family were lighthouse keepers for over 30 years but because Mum didn't speak to her mother for about 30 years we didn't know much about her side of the family. I pieced a lot of the information together later in life and, in fact, learnt more much later.

Her grandfather started as a lighthouse keeper at Puysegur Point when a ship ran aground and some of his children pulled the survivors out. He later bought a farm at Kākā Point in South Otago.

Mum and her mother had a big fight in the 1960s — they never spoke again for the rest of my grandmother's life. They were serious sulkers. Mum really only ever talked about her sister and nephews and nieces, but I heard her once talking about cousins called the McIntoshes at Kākā Point.

It wasn't until recently that I met any of Mum's cousins. It happened when I went over to the hospital to visit Aunty Tillie, who was from the West Coast. She'd had a leg amputated. When I went to her room, she was asleep, so I thought, I'll just go to the cafeteria, have a cup of coffee and come back in about half an hour.

While I was there, the partner of a woman I used to work with at Te Rūnanga o Ngāi Tahu saw me and came to sit with me. We were talking when a Pākehā girl came up and asked, 'Excuse me. Are you Mark Solomon?'

'Yes,' I said.

'Well, I'm your cousin on your mother's side, one of the Parks.'

We got talking, and after she left Trudy's partner said, 'Mark, the McIntoshes? That's my mum's family, so we must be related.'

Mum's maternal grandmother is a full Dane. I've got these lumps on my hands on both sides that are genetic. They indicate Viking blood in my whakapapa. I was at a conference in Scandinavia and shook hands with someone who recognised the lumps immediately.

Whānau

The first person who got me involved tribally was Trevor Howse, who was the Kaikōura representative on the Ngāi Tahu council at that stage. He was known as the tribal archivist.

One day, when I was in Christchurch, Trevor phoned me. I didn't even really know who he was back then. 'Come round to my house,' he said.

'I hear you're interested in whakapapa,' he said.

'Yes,' I said.

'Well, I'm not going to show you your Kaikōura side because that's the mana your family stands on.' He handed me a stack of whakapapa, and said, 'In there is your grandfather, Rangi. Come back when you've found him.'

I quickly found him, but I wanted to find other manuscripts that would support his whakapapa. It took me about three years to get what I would call the proof of his whakapapa, and I took it back to Trevor. I also took some other whakapapa that he hadn't known because I found a lot about my grandfather from the Mormon church, which stunned me.

My neighbour, who was a Mormon, had told me about the library the Mormon church has on Fendalton Road in Ōtautahi, so she got me an appointment and I went in. All they had was one microfiche film, which had on it Kahungunu whakapapa with some Ngāi Tahu towards the end. Ngāti Kahungunu share some whakapapa with Ngāi Tahu.

I put the microfiche into the reader and wound it. When I stopped, there was my grandfather and grandmother's wedding certificate on the screen. And then the next one was all of my grandfather's descent lines from Tutukawa, a Ngāi Tahu ancestor.

How the Mormon church got the information I don't know, because my ancestors have never been tied in with the Mormons.

One weekend when I was at home at Takahanga Marae, Aunty Wharetutu, my dad's older sister, said,

‘I hear you’ve been looking at the whakapapa? Tai, go and get one of those rolls of white paper, please.’

Tai Stirling was her son and my cousin. When he brought in a roll of paper, she chucked it on the ground.

‘There,’ she said. ‘If you think you know them, write them up.’

Because I was young and confident, I said, ‘Oh, yeah? Do I go back to Rangi and Papa?’ Ranginui and Papatūānuku are the beginning of life. Rangi is the sky, the father of all things; Papa is the earth, the mother of all things.

After I had written down the whakapapa, she said, ‘Tai, go home and get all the books and give them to your cousin. Mark, you’re now the kaitiaki.’

She handed it all to me that day. Becoming kaitiaki of the family whakapapa is not something to be taken lightly. Knowing who you come from, and therefore where, is very important in te ao Māori, or the Māori world. Whakapapa is a fundamental part of our culture that says who we are, places us in a wider context and links us to places and people.

I got all of our whakapapa through a back door, actually. I heard on the grapevine that my grandmother’s surviving sister had demanded a copy of all of her mother's manuscripts. So I called her up. 'Aunty Eva, would you mind if I came down for the weekend to have a look at Nanny's manuscripts?'

'Oh, don't be silly,' she said. 'I'll photocopy them and send them to you.' That's how, to my delight, I ended up with the documents of my great-grandmother Hariata, who was renowned as an important leader of Ngāti Kurī.

Whakapapa is family. When you have a Māori father and a Pākehā mother, there are definitely differences in the way that both peoples look at things. Mum's idea of family was her sister and her children. But my dad would say about someone, 'Oh, this is a close relation of yours.' We'd say, 'How do you mean a close relation?'

'Well, their great-great-great-grandmother and your great-great-great-grandfather were brother and sister,' he'd say. Even at that distance, you're still considered family.

Family, to me, is about the nuclear family. Whānau is about the extended family — and there is a difference. One of the things that got me hooked into whakapapa was when I was earwigging one day as my grandfather was telling my aunty off because she'd run down a Ngāi Tahu family.

I can still remember him saying to her, 'The trouble with you is you have no idea who you are. It doesn't matter which Ngāi Tahu family you run down; you're running yourself down because we are a tribe of cousins.'

That really hooked me. I used to use that statement a lot in my talks as kaiwhakahaere. In my role, I literally worked for 65,000 cousins.

Mum's family was from Dunedin, and we used to see our grandfather on her side once a year, I suppose. But with Dad's family, we were up in Ōaro at every opportunity. Even though Mum and Dad built a house in Belfast, just north of Christchurch, in 1961, they never called it home. Home was Ōaro. Even Mum called Ōaro home. Belfast was just a place I lived as a kid.

We wouldn't go to Ōaro every weekend because Dad was a taxi driver then, and the weekends were when you made big money, especially if you were on night shift. He had started out driving trams, then buses in the 1950s; he bought a taxi in the early 1960s. But every opportunity we had, we were in Ōaro.

Dad had a 1938 Studebaker, which was an

awesome car. All of us would be in the car, three kids in the back and one in the front with Mum and Dad. There were a lot more one-way bridges on the way from Ōtautahi to Ōaro in those days than there are now. In fact, they were all one-way bridges, really. One day, we came down through the Hawkswood Cut, north of Parnassus, and the whole hill was on fire. We had to drive through the flames. That was exciting.

Kaikōura and Ōaro have always been home for me, even though the Solomons are not from there. The Solomons are from Koukourārata, or Port Levy, on Banks Peninsula. When my grandfather married my grandmother, he moved up to Ōaro. That's why, although I fully know my connections with Koukourārata, home is up the line at Ōaro. This is where all my good memories are from. We had a big extended family and lots of cousins around my age.

There was only one male member of the line, my grandfather's father, and all his sisters married and moved out of Koukourārata. My grandfather's mother died in Ōaro. She's buried up at home. His dad's buried out at Tuahiwi.

I've always believed that the marriages of my grandfather's aunties were very strategic. Ngāi Tahu families like the Tikaos have our whakapapa; the Manawatus have our whakapapa, the Rurus have our whakapapa, right through to the Pitamas.

I suppose you'd call the Tikao family the mātāmua, or the first line, because the older Solomon, Hana, married Taare Tikao.

The Tikao line comes from Kaikōura, originally. Well, all Ngāi Tahu do because that was a staging post for the Ngāi Tahu migration from Te Ika a Māui. Kaikōura was occupied first. There are a lot of different lines that make us Ngāi Tahu, but there are three main lines of descent — that is, Waitaha, Māmoe and Tahu.

Ko ō mātou kāinga
nohoanga, ko ā mātou
mahinga kai, me waiho
mārie mō ā mātou tamariki,
mō muri iho i a mātou.

Our places of residence,
cultivations and food-
gathering places must still
be left to us, for ourselves
and our children after us.

Childhood

I had an awesome upbringing. The only negative in my life was when my dad died when I was 12. The aunty I was closest to was my Aunty Jane, my dad's younger sister. She also died young.

There were four of us kids: me, my older brother, Wayne, and my two younger sisters, Rana and Keri, who died at the age of 21. She took cyanide and committed suicide.

Before we moved to Belfast, we lived in Aranui, which is on the eastern side of the city, towards the coast. It has always been the poorer side of Ōtautahi. Our part of Aranui was known as Sandy Lands. There was our street, then all sand dunes. That was our playground, the sand dunes. There was a bit of grass on them, lupins and so on, but it was basically just sand dunes. And I should know: I once got buried in them, up to my neck, as a punishment from my brother.

The first school I went to, in 1959, was Linwood Primary. To get there was a tram ride, a penny each way. My brother and I would catch the tram to school but at the end of the day we would use our penny for the fare home to buy lollies and walk home. The tram ride took about 10 minutes and it took about three-quarters of an hour to walk, but you could get a big bag of lollies for a penny.

When Mum and Dad bought the section out in Belfast and built a house there, I moved to Belfast Primary. I will always remember my first teacher at Belfast, Mrs Caldwell, who was affectionately known as the Dragon. We were terrified of her. She ruled with a three-foot ruler. She would get your knuckles just like that.

I liked school. I had a good time there and even though Mrs Caldwell was a dragon, she and Mr Burt, another teacher, were amazing storytellers. Everyone I've known who was in Mrs Caldwell's class is a prolific reader. I credit her with a lot of my knowledge because she gave us all a love of reading.

My family were all great readers. I think that reading so much throughout my life has really helped form my ideas. Even now, when I go up home to Ōaro, my way to relax is with a book.

I had really good times at Belfast Primary and then went to Papanui High, which I hated. I think I thought I was ready to go to work, but damn, I had to go to high school.

When I was younger, I knocked around with a guy called Chris Stevens, who lived up the road. I spent a lot of time with the Stevens family, with Chris, Brian and Sandra. To avoid being made to do jobs, we would disappear on our bikes as soon as we got up. We'd bike everywhere, out to Woodend or Kairaki. We never hung around at home. If you stayed at home, you were given jobs to do. If you disappeared, you didn't get anything until you got home.

I don't remember any racism towards me, but I do remember that when my father bought our house he couldn't get household insurance unless he could prove that he was less than a half-caste Māori.

Dad

When my dad, George, died in 1966, when I was just 12, it was a bit of a shock. He was only 39. He had a double heart attack and the second one killed him. He was meant to go to Greenlane Hospital in Auckland before Christmas to have a bypass but he put it off because of Christmas. He was going to go in January instead. Well, he died on 2 December 1966.

There was a big, tall guy sitting beside me at his tangi, crying.

'What are you crying for?' I asked him.

'That's my father,' he said.

'No, it's not. It's my father,' I said.

That's how I discovered my brother, John Bond.

He was older than me, and he was the only kid who had a bike at Ōaro. No one had ever told me he was my brother.

I went to all my uncles and aunties at the tangi and said, 'That guy over there reckons he's my brother.'

Go and ask your mother, they told me. 'Mum, that guy over there says he's my brother,' I said to her.

'Yes, he's your father's eldest son,' she said. It turned out that Dad had other children to another woman.

My grandmother refused to have Dad's casket opened for the tangi, probably because he had always been very fussy about his looks. Whenever my grandfather arrived and got out of his car, Dad would pull his coat off so he could brush it for him. We used to all get lined up for him to check that we were tidy enough to go out. It was an inspection. And if we didn't have two showers a day, we were just dirty little animals. He had a fetish for cleanliness, if I can put it that way.

There are some unusual stories about my dad. There was once this old lady at a tangi, dressed to the hilt. She looked like a million dollars. She sat down beside me and said, 'Are you George Solomon's son?'

'Yeah,' I said.

'Oh, I loved your father,' she said. 'Your father was one of the most magnificent musicians I've ever known.'

'What?' I replied. 'I didn't know my dad could play a musical instrument.'

'I'm not talking about a musical instrument, dear,' she said.

Oh, lady, I thought. Too much information.

At another tangi, a lady sitting beside me asked, 'Are you George Solomon's son?'

'Yes,' I said.

'Do you know your father's nickname?'

'What was it?' I asked, like a fool.

'Your dad was known as the Bull.'

Given that I had just found out I had an older brother, I suppose I could accept that, I said.

'Oh, it wasn't that, dear.'

'Well then, why was he called the Bull?'

'Because of all the cows that chased him.'

Work

I got my first job in 1969, when I was 16. I had conned my mother into allowing me to have a Christmas job at the Borthwicks Freezing Works, where Mum worked in the cafeteria. She knew the union delegate on the slaughter board, and so I got a role there. When I got my first weekly pay packet, there was $96 inside, at a time when the average wage was $64. I came home and said, 'Look at this, Mum. I ain't going back to school.' I was six foot two and a half inches, and weighed 18 stone. There wasn't a hell of a lot my mother could do.

'Oh, you have to,' she said. 'Your father would have never let you leave school without qualifications.'

'Well, he isn't here,' I said. 'I'm leaving school, Mum. I'm not going back.'

My first job at the works was as a labourer on the gut table. The butchers would gut the sheep and I would either be ringing, which is cutting out the anus, or after the gut was put on the table, I'd be stripping the kidneys and liver off. Or I'd be on a machine that would cut through the chest bones so you could get the lungs and heart out. There were about five roles on the gut table and you rotated every 20 minutes. It was a good job. I did four seasons, and during the last season I was being trained up as a butcher. I cruised in a sort of drunken haze for a few years. Not that I was ever good at the drinking.

The night before I started, my mother said, 'You better sit down. I have something to tell you. When you get to the freezing works, you might meet a family by the name of Crofts and they might tell you that you've got a younger brother. I don't know if it's true. Your father's not here anymore to defend himself or not, but they might say something.'

This was a bit like meeting my older half-brother, but I didn't get much more information from her.

The next day I was taken onto the slaughter board by a board walker. As I walked onto the board, someone said, 'Hey, Solomon. Do you know you've got a younger brother?'

'Yeah, I do, thank you,' I said. 'My mum told me last night, but thanks for bringing it up.' Whoa. There was so much information about my family that seemed to be mentioned as an afterthought, and so many things I didn't know about my dad.

I enjoyed the freezing works because it seemed to be a microcosm of New Zealand, but I didn't think of the works as a real job because it was seasonal and you always had to find something in the off-season. In the first off-season, I did shearing. I went out with a blade-shearing gang who used the old hand blades instead of the electric. Some of the shearers were amazing. They'd do 360 to 380 sheep a day.

It's the only job I've ever been sacked from. I was the presser, pressing the wool, and so part of my job was to make sure that the pens were full for the shearers. This wool classer kept yelling out, 'Pen,' which meant the pens needed more sheep for the shearers. I'd stop to go and move them, only to discover that all of the pens had sheep, and yet he did it all morning. When it came to lunchtime, he said, 'You can work through because you're behind.'

'I'm not working through,' I said. 'You've messed me around all morning.'

'You're sacked,' he said.

'Suit yourself,' I said, and I walked out. As I came out of the hut with my gear, the farmer saw me and asked, 'What are you doing?'

I explained that I had been sacked because I had refused to work through lunch.

'Come with me,' the farmer said, and he took me straight into the dining room, and up to the classer. 'Get off my farm,' the farmer said to him.

'What?'

'You heard me. You've pissed this boy around all morning and then you sack him because he wouldn't work through lunch. Get off my farm.'

'You,' the farmer said to me. 'Get back to work.'

I had been sacked for 20 minutes. That's the only period of unemployment in my life.

The gang boss was an Irishman. I'd been out on the gang with him for three months when one day he said, 'Mate, what religion are you?'

'I'm a Catholic,' I said. The bloke never spoke to me again. Later, he told me I wouldn't be re-employed the next season.

'Well, good,' I replied. 'I don't want to come back. Your type of bigotry is bloody ridiculous.' Anybody who ditches someone because of their religion is an idiot, as far as I'm concerned.

Pāua

When I was a kid, we used to pull big pāua up. When I tell my kids how many pāua there were, and how big they were, they think I'm a liar, but they were way bigger than my hand. The pāua, that is. I reckon there are actually just as many pāua on the Kaikōura coastline today as there were back then, but the only difference is that you now find them 20 feet deeper.

After the shearing gang, I did a couple of seasons of commercial pāua diving in the off-season from the freezing works. I loved diving for pāua. The Ministry of Fisheries had recently issued permits to regions and there were 12 issued to the Kaikōura coastline. My grandfather, Rangi, totally opposed the idea of commercialising the areas through permits, which were really the forerunner of quota, and he tried to buy all the licences but only managed to buy 10, so he couldn't stop it. He gave me and another cousin a permit, so I did a couple of seasons up there diving.

It was absolutely amazing money. On one dive, I earned $986. And I had a lot of good experiences. One day, I got taken around to this spot by Uncle Johnny and did the dive on the tide. He just sat on the boat. Every time I'd come up to the surface and look up at him, he'd be laughing. When I had finished the dive and was back in the boat, I said, 'What have you been laughing at? Every time I have a look you're giggling.'

He pointed. There was a basking shark in the water.

'That shark's gone over you at least a dozen times and I've been waiting to hear you scream from under the sea,' he said.

'Never mind a scream. I would have shit myself,' I said. I had never even seen a shadow.

Another day, I was out on the boat crayfishing with Uncle Johnny at the same spot. As I was pulling the pot up on the winch, the boat started to rock and I heard my uncle go, 'Fuck.' When I turned around,

I was looking straight into the eye of a whale. There was a massive wound on top of its head, and it looked like something had taken a big bite out it. It had just come in close to shore to nurse. It rocked the boat, did its breath and then dived. Amazing.

One day, my grandfather and I chopped up a giant squid that had washed up against his slipway, the full body. We filled 16 cases with its tentacles and body. Some of them have big hooks, but this one had suckers and teeth on its tentacles.

Koro

I always explain to my kids that my grandfather, Rangi Solomon, was the most human human being I ever knew. He was so caring. I suppose now we would say that he had a highly developed EQ or emotional intelligence.

My grandparents and my uncles were very fair-minded people. My grandparents always taught me that true rangatiratanga was about service, not about being the boss. You are the spokesperson for the people.

One day, my grandfather and I had been to a meeting at Tuahiwi, north of Ōtautahi. On the way back, I asked him, 'Whenever you speak Māori, you translate it all. Why?'

He said, 'Well, there were two people in that room who speak Māori. Yes, it's appropriate that we speak te reo, but what's the point if no one understands what we're saying? And so, I translate.'

None of us was brought up speaking te reo Māori. My understanding is that my oldest aunty and my dad had te reo as kids, but they didn't continue with it once they started school. At that stage, it was considered advantageous to use te reo Pākehā. One day, I asked my grandfather about that. 'So, Grandad,' I said. 'Is it true what they say, that it's the education system that lost the language?'

'No. No, I don't agree with that at all,' he said. 'If you wish to blame someone, blame my generation and my parents. We decided it was important that our children be educated in the Pākehā system because it would put food on the table, give them a job and put a roof over their head. If anything, we took it too far. But those who blame it all on the education system, what they consistently forget is that no one ever came into homes and said, "You can't speak in te reo." Yes, your father and that would be strapped if they spoke Māori in school, but they weren't there to learn Māori.'

These days, they don't teach Mandarin or

Cantonese in school, but the children of a lot of the new immigrants still speak other languages. There was nothing to prevent Māori from doing that. I think it's become an excuse. That's just my personal opinion and it was Grandad's, too. I think te reo is important and it is great that so many rangatahi speak te reo and that so many people want to speak te reo now, especially after all those years of trying to get rid of our language. I can understand it much better than I can speak it. Even after all this time I am not confident expressing my ideas in te reo.

Listen

I've always tried to model myself on how my Uncle Johnny, my Uncle Bill and my grandfather acted, especially after Dad's death. Uncle Bill taught me to listen carefully. One day, I was having a moan to him about someone and asked why he put up with him.

'The man's an idiot,' I said, 'and ninety per cent of what comes out of his mouth is pure crap.'

What I got back from Uncle Bill was, 'Trouble with you, you don't know how to listen. We all know that every now and again out of that man's mouth drops a pure diamond. We wait to hear the tinkle. Learn to listen, boy.'

Three weeks later, I had to phone him. 'Guess what, Uncle Bill? I heard the tinkle of the diamond today.'

'Told you,' he said. 'Learn to bloody listen.'

I got another good lesson from Jono Crofts, the Ngāi Tahu elder, when I went out to a hui at Tuahiwi, in the middle of winter. They had turned the heaters on but it was still so cold inside that as people were talking all you could see was the condensation from their breath. After they had welcomed me, I stood up with my coat on to respond. When we were doing the hongi and the harirū, I got up to Jono and he said, 'Are you in a hurry, boy?'

'No, why?' I asked.

'You got your coat on. Looks like you're ready to run.'

'It's freaking freezing, Jono.'

'No, no,' he said. 'It looks like you're ready to run.'

Three months later, there was a Ngāi Tahu meeting at Ōraka Aparima at the bottom of Te Waipounamu, right on the southern coast. It was brutally cold. When it was my turn to talk, I stood up and took my coat off. I could hear a kid behind me saying to his grandmother, 'What's he taking his coat off for? It's freezing.'

His tāua said, 'He's showing respect to the people, boy.'

Ko te toa i a tini i a
mano o te tangata.

We possess the strength
of the many. It is the
bravery of a multitude, of
thousands of people.

Ōaro

My memories of my childhood are just like anybody else's. On a school day, I'd get up. Weet-Bix and Kornies were the favourites for breakfast. We had to do the dishes. We had to make our beds before school. We had to make our lunches. If you were too lazy to make your lunch, you went hungry.

We had jobs. I used to do lawns, only because I liked it. Mum and Dad were pretty hard. Can I have a bike for Christmas? Of course, you can, my boy. Get a job.

Uncle Bill bought us our first TV because he lived with us when we were young. I remember my first TV programme, *Wagon Train*. Best TV programme I saw. At Ōaro, they had bought a TV but you couldn't see the picture; all you got was snow, because the reception was so bad. They knew every ad jingle and they knew all the theme songs, but you just couldn't see a picture. My cousins would be sent outside to climb the roof to move the aerial when there was a southerly blowing.

The uncles were funny. Once, when we were kids, Uncle Johnny asked me, my brother Wayne, and our cousin Ned to dig a long-drop toilet. Well, we three dummies forgot to ask how much he would pay us. It had to be a minimum of six foot deep. It took us three days. When we had finished, Uncle Johnny came out to inspect it.

'A magnificent job,' he said and gave us two bob each. 'Top job, top job. I'll even give you a bonus. Two bob for you, two bob for you.'

We couldn't believe it.

'What? We've spent three days digging this for two bob each?' we said.

'I was only going to give you one and six, so you've had a bonus,' he said.

We were so furious we went back that night and filled it in. Uncle Johnny had to dig it out again, but at least we had done the hard digging for him.

I remember the day we all got three haircuts. Grandad used hand clippers and they were painful. I reckon he took more skin than he took hair. We all got a bowl placed on our heads and were given a bowl cut. We hated it. We went over to see Uncle Vic, who told us to stop moaning.

'Oh, you long-haired louts. Sit down.' And we got another haircut. Then we went to Uncle John and he did the same.

When we were at home at Ōaro, we just lived off the land. Every bach in those days had fruit trees — the whole place was a garden. There were wars over the fruit: the Solomons versus the Nortons, who were our cousins at Ōaro. They weren't allowed to touch our fruit. It was allowed to rot on the ground but they weren't allowed to eat it.

My grandparents had a quarter acre. It was all fruit trees. They had three different types of cherries, a couple of types of apricots, peaches, greengages, apples, plums. We all remember one plum tree that was outside the kitchen. When you bit the plums they exploded with juice. Years later, I found a tree up on our farm that hadn't been pruned for years, so the fruit was only small, but it's the same plum variety.

I've got a loquat tree on my property that my great-grandfather planted. I've also got old, old-style plum trees. There are some pear trees that are well over 100 years old. They're still alive, still fruiting. They're pretty rugged.

We used to have an apple up there called a Black Prince, which had black skin and a glassy centre. My great-grandfather had a mandarin–grapefruit graft that he'd grafted himself; you could eat them like oranges. He was marvellous at fruit trees.

Urupā

My first role of responsibility in the family was at the age of 23, when I was put in charge of all burials at Ōaro. In my time doing that, until I handed it over in 2007, I buried 26 of my family.

The urupā at Ōaro is called Pā Ngaio and it is very old. In the 1990s, Professor David Nobes from Canterbury University explored the urupā using a shallow electromagnetic magnetometer and ground-penetrating radar techniques. It was called a geophysical survey and is ideal for non-invasive exploration, for discovering what is there while leaving the site intact. There were older graves at Pā Ngaio but no one knew where they were because the makers and oral record had been lost.

When David came up and surveyed our urupā, we found that what we thought was the urupā was only a part of it. There had been burials all down the sides of the hill. One body was found plugged in the ground, standing upright.

It's an amazing urupā but the soil is incredibly hard. Eventually, I decided we should stop digging graves by hand and use a digger. The first time we brought a digger in, the driver put the bucket on, lifted it, slammed it and only got about a quarter of an inch into the clay.

'Shit,' he said. 'You mean to tell me you have been digging this by hand?'

'Yep,' I said.

A lot of the cousins worked on the railways, so later on we would use jackhammers from their work. When my grandfather died, it only took two hours to dig his grave using them.

Digging a grave by hand is brutal work. The first grave we dug was my grandmother's, in May 1977. In typical fashion, our uncles told us to get up the hill and start work. 'You lot, get up that bloody hill and dig our mother's grave,' they told my brother and some cousins and me. 'Make sure you do a good job. It's our mother.' Those were our instructions. So we plodded up the hill.

It took us 16 hours. It was unbelievably hard. My older brother said to me, 'We need water. You can go and get it.'

There was no road to the urupā and you had to walk over the hill to get water. When I came back with the water, he came out to me with his hand extended.

'Congratulations,' he said. 'While you were away, we had a meeting. You're now in charge of all burials.'

'Don't I get a say?' I asked.

'Nah, you would have lost. It was unanimous. Now here's your first job.'

'I thought I was in charge,' I said.

'Yeah, right,' he said. 'Tell those three to come and give us a hand.'

Three of our cousins were down the hill sitting in front of what used to be the schoolhouse at Ōaro, in their suits, laughing at everyone up on the hill. So down I went.

'See your cousins up on the hill there?' I said. 'If you're not up there in 15 minutes, if one of you was to die, you'll have to bury yourselves. You're either part of the family or you're not.'

They were up there in 15 minutes and digging. When we got down to the four-foot mark, we hit a rock wider than the grave and we had to split it. It was massive.

For me, the final part of the tangi was filling in the grave. I didn't like having a sexton do it, and for me the closure of a death was that actual physical act of filling the grave. After that, all the emotions of the tangi would hit me. I knew I had a role to do, and once it was done, the emotions would hit.

I could not come back from digging the grave and then go and sit on the paepae of the marae. The gravedigger does not sit on the paepae. Because I was part of the burial, I was tapu, set apart.

I'm now banned from burials at Koukourārata, not allowed to ever dig there again, because I've hit bodies when I've been digging. They're spooky, all of them. When one aunty died, we went over to Koukourārata to dig with the whānau. As we started digging, I said, 'This doesn't feel right. This is funny ground. It's too soft.' We dug a little more and found the remains of a woman. We thought she must have been someone from after settler contact because she had glasses and a pearl necklace; the clasp was two hands that locked. She was wrapped in sack. We rang the police and said, 'This is not a family burial.' But they refused to come and investigate so we just reburied her.

When we came off the hill, I was told, 'This is the

last time you're ever allowed to dig on our urupā.'

I said, '*Our* urupā? You're the same family.'

'You're not burying here,' they said. 'You're banned.'

I handed over to our kids' generation in 2007, when my cousin died. He was the first of us grave-diggers to die. I said to my lot, 'We're all in our fifties. It's time we brought the next generation on.'

All of us older men were convinced the young people wouldn't turn up. But about thirty arrived and they blitzed us.

Maria

The first time I saw the woman I would marry, I was 17 and at kapa haka, up home in Kaikōura. It would have been 1971. I was a smoker back then and we'd stopped for a break. I was outside having a fag when this girl walked past with her boyfriend. And I just knew she would become my wife.

I guess it could have been love at first sight, although that doesn't really explain the certainty that I felt. I knew from the first moment. In fact, I didn't even speak to her. She was walking past with her boyfriend, and I was with my cousin, Martin Manawatu, or Ned, as we called him. 'See that girl there, Ned?' I asked him. 'That's my wife.'

'How do you know?' Ned asked, which of course

was a perfectly reasonable thing to ask.

'I just know,' I said.

Everyone in Kaikōura played darts and I met her again at a darts do. Two years later, in October 1974, we got married in a Presbyterian church, her church. She was 15 minutes late because her father took the wedding car driver for a tour of his garden.

'Where the hell have you been?' I whispered to her at the altar.

'Dad had to show the driver the garden,' she said.

For years afterwards, every time we'd go home to some of my aunties, they'd say, 'Now, you two, when are you getting married?'

'We are married,' I'd say.

'We mean in a proper church.'

They meant a Catholic church, of course, and we did redo our vows later in a Catholic church.

The night after I was elected kaiwhakahaere, I had only been home in Christchurch for half an hour when the phone rang. It was Lady Sandra O'Regan, the wife of Tā Tipene O'Regan, who himself was a former chair of the trust board and was the man responsible for getting Te Kerēme, as the Ngāi Tahu claim was known, over the line. He has given years of his life to Ngāi Tahu.

'Bring your wife around to my house immediately,' she said. Click.

I said to Maria, 'We're going out.' So, we went round to Sandra's house and knocked on the door.

'Come in, please,' Sandra said to Maria. 'I've asked Mark to bring you round so you understand what he's got you into. He thinks he's got a job of chairing a meeting once a month. I'm telling you, this job absolutely consumes you. He will miss every one of your children's birthdays and yours. You will no longer be able to go out as a couple without people sitting down to talk to you. He will miss your wedding anniversary. He'll miss everything. In fact, you are now a solo mother.'

'I thought it was just chairing a meeting once a month,' I said to Maria on the way home. 'Just say, and I'll chuck it in.'

'No, no, no. I'll look after the kids,' she said. 'You look after the tribe.'

I soon found out that Lady Sandra was right. I did miss so much over the years as kaiwhakahaere. I was constantly away on iwi matters. And I was constantly involved in dealing with Crown breaches of our settlement, things like not always offering Ngāi Tahu the first right of refusal on parcels of Crown land when they come available. Tipene had been right when he told me that it would never be over, that the settlement would always be redefined.

To me, Maria's a real matriarch. She runs the family. I mean that in a positive way. She's definitely the pou or the rock of our family, more so than I am. My kids don't come to me; they go to their mother. They come to me when they want money. Their nickname for me is 'Wallet', and my daughter has described me as a financial necessity.

Maria was 17 and I was 20 when we got married, and we had our first child three years later. We've been married for 46 years. I've been incredibly lucky. I knew from the moment I saw her that we would be together.

Foundryman

Because I was getting married, I thought I had better get a real job, a full-time job. So I applied for a role as a metal buyer for an Aussie company called Copper Refining and Chemical Company, which was a scrap metal outfit and a foundry.

About six weeks after I started, the father of the foreman of the foundry died. The boss called me in to his office and said, 'Would you give it a go? We've got to try to keep production up while he's away at his father's funeral.'

This guy used to start at three o'clock in the morning and he would finish at seven at night. I said to the boss, 'Look, I'm willing to give it a go. But I've just got married. I'm not starting at three in the morning and finishing at seven at night. Here's the deal. I'll give it a go. I'll start at six a.m. But I walk out of the factory at five p.m.'

And he said, 'Deal.'

The first day in the role, I had to do three half-ton melts. A melt is the mixture of scrap metal that you had to do. You put in about 545 kilograms and by the time it's all melted down and you've taken all the dross off, you get back about 520 kilograms per melt. I knew nothing about it but immediately thought, Well, if I'm going to be melting metal, it would make sense to put the lighter stuff in first, because that would melt the quickest and then create a pool of molten metal. I just worked it out for myself.

The foundryman did it the opposite way. He would put all the heavy stuff in first and the light stuff in last. Hence, he was starting at three, finishing at seven. My way was much, much quicker.

I walked into the boss's office at 2.30 p.m. on that first day and said, 'Finished.'

'You've what?' he said disbelievingly.

'I've done the three melts,' I said.

'What are your weights?' he asked. I gave him the weights.

'As of today, you are the foreman of the foundry,' he said.

I got a lot of advice from old foundrymen. Some of them were amazing. I used to deal a lot with an old guy down on Dyers Pass Road in Ōtautahi who taught me how to judge the temperature of molten metal by the colour. I used his methodology for about eight years until we got all high-tech and went out and bought a pyrometer, which is simply a copper wire that has asbestos over it. You just dip it into the molten metal and it gives you an electronic reading of the temperature. I could get the temperature by colour, guessing within 10 degrees every time because I had been taught so well. This old guy was frigging amazing.

I used to make up mixtures of scrap metal. Had my own little formulas. A lot of the foundries we supplied would only take certified metals. So if they bought what they called LG2, it was made up of 85 per cent copper, 5 per cent tin, 5 per cent lead, 5 per cent zinc, 0.1 maximum of iron. Just by making mixtures of scrap metal, I averaged 94 per cent in spec on LG2 and 96 per cent in valve metal, which is what you get from big gate bells, et cetera. I could get a 96 per cent success rate by scrap metal mixtures, which was pretty good. They used to send samples to A. W. Fraser, out at Lunns Road. There was a spectrograph there, and they did the analysis of the metals.

I worked in foundries for 25 years and had some incredible near misses. How I never killed myself I'm not sure, but the working conditions were shocking. I had a boss who I think thought it was cheaper to kill a person than buy better equipment. That was just the attitude back then. One day, I was using a refractory to make the linings of the furnaces when a salesman came in and said, 'What are you doing working with this without respirators?'

I said, 'Why?'

'That stuff is highly carcinogenic.' It was news to me.

'Show me the warnings,' I said. There was nothing on the label. I said, 'I've been using this stuff for about fourteen bloody years. There's no health warnings, nothing that comes with it.' But this stuff was in fact as bad as asbestos.

Then Occupational Health and Safety regulations came in and all of a sudden a new line of products came out with all the warnings. I'd worked for years without a clue.

I vividly remember one explosion that almost killed me. One day, I forgot to open a massive gate valve on the furnace. A furnace is made up of a quarter-inch plate inside 6 inches of refractory. Then inside the refractory is a carbon silicate crucible. This gate valve exploded, and when it exploded it split the furnace. All the molten metal went sideways, and as the gate valve itself split, it came out of the furnace and brushed my head on both sides, blowing me off my feet. I was deaf for about 20 minutes.

I had always thought that eventually a lung disease would get me. I was a heavy smoker and I worked in a foundry. It was an industry where we had to be blood tested every month for lead poisoning.

It's certainly not the easiest process if you do get lead poisoning, because it gets into your bones. The only way to get rid of it is to have a blood transfusion. You could get it done in the morning, be tested that afternoon and the lead levels were back within the safety limits. Next day, another blood test and you're way back up high again.

It didn't help that I also used to make racing keels for yachts, which were full of lead, and which could be really dangerous to work with. There were some amazing explosions doing that and it was another way in which I nearly got killed. One day, I had a four-and-a-half-ton keel to pour. The mould was made out of concrete and a heater was built into the concrete to help it set. It was so hot that you couldn't touch the concrete without getting burnt. That day, I thought, There's no way there's going to be any moisture in this, so I'll do a fast pour. I was about half an inch from the top when the whole thing exploded — four and a half ton of lead went up and outwards. But I never got so much as a splash.

A similar thing happened on an aluminium furnace. Lead and aluminium are the worst metals to work with because if you get a splash it will solidify and stick as soon as it touches your skin. When this furnace exploded, it just went straight up. Once again, I took a step back and the whole thing dumped in front of me. So again, not so much as a splash burn.

The worst burn I saw happen was when I was teaching a young guy. I said to him, 'Look, you can put some water in the top of the aluminium. See, it just steams up. But you can never put anything in it that seals both ends. You've always got to open one of the ends before you put it in.'

I showed him a couple of pieces. 'This is the sort of stuff I mean. See how it's sealed at both ends? You can never put that in a furnace without opening one. I'm going to go and have a cup of tea. You know what to do. I'll see you in 15 minutes.'

I had hardly gone a few metres when there was a massive explosion, then a scream. He'd put one of the sealed pieces in and as soon as it hit the liquid it just exploded, and the metal came up onto his watch and instantly solidified. By the time I was able to snap off his watch, all the skin on his wrist had burnt away. He was off work for about six months.

Another incident was weirder. It happened to a guy who was a great worker but did not like doing up his boots. Well, there was an explosion and big dollops of molten metal went straight down inside his boot and he couldn't get his boot off. That was a terrible burn. If he'd had his boots done up, he would have been fine.

Mana

You inherit mana through your past: 'Hey, this is the grandson of Rangi Solomon who was on the Ngāi Tahu Māori Trust Board.' My grandfather was a tribal strategist. So you inherit mana through people like him.

The other mana is given to you by your actions. You don't earn mana, in my opinion. It's given.

My grandfather Rangi and my uncles, Bill and Johnny, were always what I would call my litmus tests, especially after my dad died. They certainly were pivotal male role models in my life. They were good people who treated others well. Rangi was very caring. Whenever he went down to Christchurch with a load of cray tails for export, on the way home to

Ōaro he'd stop at one of the orchards out of Belfast and fill his truck with cases of apples and then drop the cases off to the families in Ōaro when he got back. He was just a good man.

When I got involved with Ngāi Tahu, I always had in mind that I would treat people how I'd like to be treated. But I also did things that others wouldn't. I used to refuse to go straight to the table during meetings, as some people did, and wait to be served kai, for example. I would get in the queue for the kai instead. I didn't feel as though I had any more rights than anyone else. And anyway, that's when people talk to you. That's when people who won't stand up in a formal meeting to ask a question will ask you a question.

Although my grandfather was on the Ngāi Tahu Māori Trust Board for years, and involved in tribal politics, my dad wasn't. Dad wasn't the slightest bit interested in tribal politics. My mum knew more about Ngāti Kurī, our hapū, than my dad did. Uncle Bill and Uncle Johnny weren't interested in tribal politics to begin with either, even though Uncle Bill ended up as the upoko, or customary head, of Ngāti Kurī. In fact, Uncle Johnny was not a public person at all. Uncle Bill was the same, although it seems hard to believe now.

After my grandfather died, there was a meeting held by the family, and it was decided that Uncle Bill, whether he liked it or not, would step up as the trust board representative for Marlborough. Not Uncle Johnny because Uncle Johnny flatly refused.

Uncle Bill was so nervous at the first meeting he attended that as he spoke, the back of the chair that he was gripping shattered. He was holding on to it that firmly.

He manawa tahi, he
manawa ora, he manawa
toa, te manawa Kāi Tahu.

A united heart, a vibrant
heart, a determined heart,
this is the heart of Kāi Tahu.

Values

I was once invited out to the Deloitte tent at the Canterbury A&P show to speak to farmers about Māori values. I had thought I was going out for a few nibbles, but the price of entry turned out to be having to get up and speak about Māori values, which some people seem to have some trouble with.

After I was introduced, I stood up and said, 'Well, I've been asked if I'd give you a talk on the Māori values. Can you hang on to your seats because you might get a bit of a fright with what I'm going to say to you. I mean, it mightn't be obvious, but I've also got Pākehā blood. Now, these values . . . when my father talked about whanaungatanga, my Pākehā mother talked about family. When my dad talked about kaitiakitanga, my Pākehā mum would talk about stewardship or guardianship. Where my dad talked about tohungatanga, my mum would talk about getting a good education. Where Dad talked about manaaki, Mum would talk about hosting and all of its aspects. This dreaded word called rangatiratanga, well, my mum would say, "You act in an honourable, chiefly manner." Real complicated, isn't it?'

Afterwards, two farmers came up to me and said, 'You know, we were expecting this big spiritual talk, but that was so bloody common sense and practical.'

I said, 'Think about it. What culture doesn't have values?'

Tapu

Tapu is a Māori concept that some people like to make more complex than I think it is. To me, it can be quite simple, but some people prefer to wrap up the concept of tapu in spiritual talk.

I remember Uncle Ku lecturing us about the concept of tapu and essentially saying that it originated for practical purposes. 'You know, this concept of tapu. People think it's all about spiritual stuff,' he said. 'But it's really about practical things. Why did you have a tapu on a garden? "Oh, you kids. Don't play in there, that's where we're growing the food. Would you people stop chucking the rubbish over the fence? That's where the garden is. Don't use it as a footpath." That's what a tapu is.'

As Uncle Ku said, tapu was often about practical things. He was also a man whose knowledge I greatly admired and respected. His full name was Kūkupa Tirikātene and he was the brother of the MP, Whetū Tirikātene-Sullivan. Uncle Ku was a widely respected Ngāi Tahu elder and also an expert in te reo Māori and tikanga, and he often came with me in later years while I was kaiwhakahaere. He was raised on the East Coast and his parents were Sir Eruera Tirikātene and Lady Ruti Tirikātene (née Solomon). He was the first Māori-language teacher at Rosehill College in Papakura and a well-known community leader in South Auckland. He was also a cultural advisor and kaumātua at Te Papa and a professor at the Manukau Institute of Technology. His nephew is the current Te Tai Tonga MP, Rino Tirikātene.

I remember Uncle Ku coming to tell us reps from the Ngāi Tahu council off after some sort of factionalism and leaking. He told us the story about the kahikatea tree, about how its shoots and roots grow out and then they twist and intertwine, and how the whole forest is linked. So, when the wind comes, they support each other. It takes a tree quite some time to actually fall, even when it's dead, because the roots keep holding it up.

Someone said, 'Oh, what a beautiful story.'

I said, 'Nah, you've just been told off. What he was saying is that we're not acting like the kahikatea and supporting each other. We're all going in different directions. Your beautiful story was his telling off.'

It was his way of gently telling us that, as representatives on the Ngāi Tahu council, we could be more like the roots of the kahikatea trees and support each other through good times and bad.

Politics

I got involved in tribal politics gradually. When my grandfather died in 1977 I was 23 and I was asked by my uncles to replace him on the Oaro M, which is the trust board that looks after our land. I refused because I wasn't interested. Two years later, both Uncle Bill and Uncle Johnny said to me, 'Look, would you go on it for one year, until we sort out who's going to represent the family?'

In 1997, I went to Uncle Bill and said, 'Remember when you and Uncle Johnny asked me to go on the Ōaro board for one year? Well, that was in 1979. It's now 1997.'

'What's your problem?' he said.

'Well, you said one year.'

'Yeah, and when you reach it, we'll tell you,' Uncle Bill said.

When I came on board, the returns were small. It now returns $136,000 a year from 3.6 hectares. We give two distributions a year, and we set aside $10,000 a year for education. It sounds like a lot but it was simply a matter of bringing the trust into the modern world. Charging market rate for leases, for example.

I was taken to my first tribal hui in 1988, two years after the Ngāi Tahu Claim had been lodged with the Waitangi Tribunal, by Trevor Howse, who at that time was the Kaikōura rep on the council. The meeting was at Arowhenua Marae near Temuka, in South Canterbury. Trevor told me to stand against the back wall and just watch whatever happened, and then to tell him what I saw. The trust board was up on the stage; all day, in and out of the side doors would come one of the old women, who would tap someone in the audience on the shoulder and take them outside. Then that person would come back and put a question to the trust board. That happened all through the day. At the end of the hui, Trevor said, 'So what did you see?'

'The old ladies,' I said. 'It seems to me that they dictate what happens, getting people to ask questions all day.'

'You got it,' Trevor said. 'If you want to get involved with this, try and get them on your side. They run the tribe.'

That was my first meeting and I became really interested. The message that came from that meeting was that we needed people to register as Ngāi Tahu because the government had asked, 'Who are you? Who do you represent? What's your role?'

So my brother and I visited all the families in Kaikōura and encouraged them to register and get involved. Register your kids, register yourself, we said. You know, the tribe's going through the settlement process.

Back then, Ngāi Tahu had 18 papatipu rūnanga representatives on its council, who were chosen for three-year terms. In 1995, when I was 41, Trevor stood down as our rep on the Ngāi Tahu table, and two cousins were to be nominated to replace him. I carpooled to the meeting where there would be a vote with Sue King, from one of the families from Mangamaunu, the small marae north of Kaikōura at a place that's probably best known around the globe for its surf break.

We were about 15 minutes out of Kaikōura when I said to Sue, 'Well, how do you think you'll go today?'

'What do you mean, Mark?' she said.

'Well, you'll be Mangamaunu's nominee,' I said. 'You've been their gopher for years.'

'No, Mark, they're not nominating me,' she said.

I was amazed by this. It seemed unfair. 'Who the hell are they frigging nominating then?'

'Shut up,' she said. 'They're nominating you.'

I was gobsmacked. I hadn't seen it coming. At that meeting, I was nominated by Sue's father and her brother. I was profusely proud that I wasn't supported by my own family. Not that they're opposed to me but my family have a very staunch view that the eldest always gets the nod. They all voted for my older cousin. The northern families of Mangamaunu put me in the position, not my own.

Coming onto the table was an awesome experience. I was nominated on the day and I won with a 47 per cent majority. My first board meeting was at Taumutu, one of the 18 Ngāi Tahu papatipu rūnanga and the home of Ngāti Moki and Te Taumutu Rūnanga, at the southern end of Te Waihora or Lake Ellesmere.

I arrived early, as I always did for meetings, and the first person I met was George Tikao, who was then the representative for Ōnuku on Horomaka, Banks Peninsula, just past Akaroa, and chair of Ōnuku Rūnanga, another of the 18 Ngāi Tahu papatipu rūnanga. At that time, I didn't know who George was. He introduced himself and said, 'You know, we are close relations. It is an honour to have you with me — sit at the table beside me.'

I was also told that day by Cath Brown, the Taumutu representative and a famous Ngāi Tahu artist who was hosting the meeting, and Ruahine Crofts, who was the Tūāhuriri representative from North Canterbury, that they would be my mentors, and that they would look after me.

It would be fair to say that I was pretty quiet for my first three or four meetings, until I got my head around what was going on. It was like going into a foreign land. I had been a labourer, although I had staff under me and I had run a foundry, but I never had been in a corporate position. So, it was about learning a lot about what all the issues were and coming up to speed with them.

In those first three years, Richard Parata was the chair of Ngāi Tahu Group Management. Richard had been a major in the British Army and a trained hostage negotiator who had spent time fighting against the IRA. Cath Brown and Ruahine Crofts used to tie him up in knots and he'd lose his cool. I went to him one day and said, 'Richard, you're meant to be a bloody trained hostage negotiator, and those two ladies run rings around you. I don't even want you to be a negotiator if I'm being kidnapped, man.'

He said, 'There's no bloody logic to those women.'

When I came on board in 1995, the Ngāi Tahu Trust Board only had about eight staff. We took a gamble that we would get Te Kerēme settled and increased the staff to over 40 before the settlement. We were pretty confident we'd get there, but at the time we had a big discussion at the table on what they call the green box versus the black box.

The black box was: shove the offer and we'll slug it out in court with the Crown. The green box was that we would cut our losses, accept what the Crown was putting up and go for it — a chance for Ngāi Tahu to move forward. The problem was that even the lawyers reckoned that if you took the Crown to court, the court would probably tell us to go back and negotiate with the Crown, so we would likely end up where we had been.

Through 10 land sales between 1840 and 1864, Ngāi Tahu had sold most of Te Waipounamu to the Crown. However, the Crown didn't keep its side of the bargain; it didn't pay the agreed price and it failed to set aside 10 per cent of the land in reserves for Ngāi Tahu. The Crown had ripped the tribe off. The tribe had been seeking justice for seven generations. Te Kerēme was lodged with the Waitangi Tribunal in 1986.

In 1997, the Ngāi Tahu Deed of Settlement was signed at Takahanga Marae in Kaikōura, and the following year, when I was elected as kaiwhakahaere, the Ngāi Tahu Claims Settlement Act was passed at Parliament in Wellington. Agreeing to the settlement was a huge thing for the Banks Peninsula hapū, who had four representatives on the Ngāi Tahu council, because the whole of the French purchase of Akaroa was excluded from it and they got nothing. They had lost 30-something thousand acres to the French. It had always been seen as a complex issue because the French insisted they had bought land from Ngāi Tahu through two deeds of sale in 1838 and 1840, while the Crown said that the French purchases were invalid.

Of course the $170 million settlement was not

equivalent to all we had lost, could never compensate for it, but at last we could move on. And I took a pragmatist's view: if we couldn't make it work with $170 million then it didn't matter how much we could have got.

Once a Treaty settlement is negotiated and agreed between the Crown and claimants, an act of Parliament is generally required to enforce the terms of the settlement. Te Rūnanga o Ngāi Tahu was formed in 1996 to establish Ngāi Tahu as a legal entity ahead of the passing of the Ngāi Tahu Claims Settlement Act. When the Te Rūnanga o Ngāi Tahu structure came through, we had a meeting at home at Kaikōura. Uncle Bill held up the document. 'You know that this is our new structure. I'd like a nomination that we accept.'

I said, 'Uncle Bill, what's on page thirty-five'?

'Well, I don't know,' he said.

'Neither do I.'

'You want to read it, don't you?' he said.

'Yeah,' I said. 'Cover to cover.'

'We're not going to have a vote today, are we?' he asked.

'Not until I've read it,' I replied. 'I'm not going to vote for something I haven't read.

I was appointed as the kaiwhakahaere in 1998, although I didn't lobby for it. I didn't even put my name forward. I was nominated on the day and I won. I call it an accident because I hadn't put my hand up for it. I was just nominated on the day by Puketeraki, a rūnanga in Otago, and jointly seconded by Ōraka Aparima and Waihopai from Murihiku, and I won.

After the election, I was having a cup of tea when one of the kaumātua said, 'Well, boy, you're pretty white, and because of your skin colour you've never seen how negative the South Island is. But now that you're the chairman of an iwi, you're in for a massive lesson in life.'

That's why later on I started doing a series of public talks around Te Waipounamu about the myths of the Treaty process, to give people information about the process, because a lot of what people think is racism is actually the result of ignorance. For example, I would ask people if they thought the Waitangi Tribunal process was free, and usually they did. They were astonished to learn that the Ngāi Tahu settlement process had cost us millions of dollars.

In 2020, I delivered a speech on racism to a bunch of churches and took questions afterwards. I got asked: Did I think New Zealand was racist? It's definitely racist, I said. Racism is present in every race and it's in all colours. It's not just white people who are racist. There are coloured people who are racist, too. But I personally think that racists are a minority in this country; they're just noisy. The sin is that everyone keeps turning their backs to racist talk and ignoring it.

In 2003, I think it was at Puketeraki in Otago, I brought the topic up at a Ngāi Tahu annual meeting and related what that kaumātua had told me about racism when I was elected kaiwhakahaere. I said, 'I'm sorry, Ngāi Tahu, I have not found it to be true. I'm not naive; every society has its bigots and racists, but they are often a noisy minority.'

When I was elected as kaiwhakahaere, all I got as a job description was that I needed to chair a meeting of the table or council once a month, to always try to bring quarterly data to the table, to bring kotahitanga, unity, to the table and to go forth and make relationships. It was a fairly loose description.

On my first day in the role, I was talking with the CEO of Te Rūnanga o Ngāi Tahu, Sid Ashton, who said, 'So I suppose you want to be on the same salary as Charlie.' Charlie Crofts was my predecessor.

'No,' I said to Sid. 'To be honest, I don't even know

if I can do this job. I've been a labourer all my life and this is a corporate entity. My wife and I both work at the moment but she is going to stay at home and look after our family while I look after the tribe. Give me the salary we earn together. I want my wife to finish working because we've still got kids in school.'

At the end of that first year, I got what I believe was a AAA-plus review and at a Te Rūnanga o Ngāi Tahu meeting they offered me a $5000 salary increase. I said no — I wanted a $50,000 increase. Sid just about had a heart attack. 'We can't do that. Can you step out of the room? The board needs to talk about this now.'

When I came back in, they offered me a $35,000 increase. I thought, Well, if that's what you can afford, I will take it. It was a 24/7 role and I was answerable to the tribe every minute of the day.

When I started attending the board meetings I felt they were speaking a foreign language, with corporate speak and acronyms all the way through. At one meeting, I got so annoyed that I stood up, stopped the meeting and gave the board a lecture on how to strip an electric furnace. And when I finished, I said to the chairman, 'Now repeat what I've said to you.'

'But I can't, Mark,' he said.

'Well, that's what it's like sitting in on your board meetings,' I said. 'You all use industry speak, every second word's an acronym. Why don't you just speak so everyone can understand you?'

It took me about six months to train the board to talk sense. And once they did, everything was pretty simple. Once I better understood the language, I could understand the processes they followed and it became a lot clearer.

A manager at Ngāi Tahu Development Corporation said to me one day, 'Mark, I'm sending some staff up to your marae to talk to your people about strategic planning. I want you to come, but I want you to just sit in the audience.'

He came up with two young Ngāi Tahu graduates who gave my lot a 45-minute lecture on strategic planning. When they finished, my uncle stood up and said, 'You two, that was the best presentation I've ever seen in my life. You've got to keep coming back here and bring us old fogies into this new business world that Ngāi Tahu is embarking on. Now, the ladies have got some kai on for you, away you go.'

As soon as the doors shut, he turned around, and said to me, 'All right, boy, what the hell were they talking about?'

I turned to the manager, who said, 'This is why I asked you to come, you needed to hear this.'

'Righto, uncle,' I said. 'Let's do an exercise. As the elders of Takahanga Marae, what would you like to see the trustees put on this marae for your generation, for your children and for your mokopuna?'

We ended up with 25 ideas on a whiteboard. I said, 'Okay, as the next part of this process, if you look at all the ideas we've put up, I want you to rank them from the most important down to the least important.'

We did that, then I said, 'There you are. There's your five-year strategic plan for the marae trustees. We'll take the first five for the next financial year. Now we've got to develop a business plan of how we're going to deliver on these five projects. And at the end of the financial year, I've got to stand in front of you at the AGM and say what we've achieved.'

'But that's simple,' he said. 'Why don't they talk like that?'

'Because they've just come out of university where they've been taught to deliver a thesis,' I said. 'And in a sense, they're still talking to the professor. They've forgotten that they are standing in front of uncle and aunty, grandma and granddad, who don't speak that language.'

The first big transaction when I became kaiwhakahaere was buying an 80 per cent shareholding in Shotover Jet, which was a listed company and an iconic brand. We did it over a phone conference, with no papers in front of us.

That night I got a phone call from my Uncle Bill. 'You idiots bought Shotover. What did you pay for it?'

'Dollar three.'

'I should take you all to bloody court,' he said.

'Why, Uncle?'

'The main shareholder of Shotover Jet is in financial trouble. Just back off, give it a couple of weeks and you'll get it for about 48 cents a share. You guys have just bailed him out.'

He may have been right but we weren't privy to that information and we had to go with what we had in front of us. We had already made the purchase and it was too late to back out of the deal. It worked out well anyway, because Ngāi Tahu took control of the company and made improvements so its value increased. After we'd purchased the 80 per cent, we kept buying shares until we forced it to delist and Ngāi Tahu took full control.

So that was our first deal. The Treaty settlement

had gone some way to help the tribe re-establish its asset base, but we needed to acquire companies like Shotover to take care of our cultural, commercial and environmental aspirations.

Ngāi Tahu Tourism has since become one of the largest tourism operators in New Zealand, hosting more than one million visitors a year — before Covid came along — across 14 businesses.

One lesson I learnt during my time as kaiwhakahaere is that politics is time-wasting crap. Time-wasting, costly crap. I don't mind challenge. Challenge is good, but it has to be constructive. What happens in New Zealand is that it becomes destructive. As a country, we tend to focus on deficits, on the things that aren't going well. I suppose it comes down to my own naivety, but when I came on to the Ngāi Tahu council, I thought everyone thought like me, that this was about us, that this is a family business in which we all supported each other. I was wrong, and the council became more divisive over time.

Ultimately, I think everything comes down to the battle between the 'We' and the 'I'. What I had at

Ngāi Tahu was a split table. I had half that I would say were 'We' people. It was about *us*; a family business or tribal business, and we were there for the greater good of the tribe. The other half were 'I' people, the kind who thought, 'I want my tribe to do this for me or for my rūnanga only.'

I will always stand firmly in the 'We' camp, but not everybody's like that. And yet, if you look at the responsibilities of the Ngāi Tahu representatives, they are to be the representative of their rūnanga, but the moment they are at that table, they are responsible for the collective, for Ngāi Tahu the iwi.

I used to take every board paper home and I'd get my instructions from the people on how I should vote on it, but there was always a proviso. We live in our splendid isolation, 160 kilometres away from our nearest marae neighbour and we sort of make our own decisions, but when you get to the table, there might be other information that you haven't even thought of. In those circumstances, I might have to change the way I vote, to deviate from what I had been told by the rūnanga. I've always had a totally open process in the way I've dealt with the home people.

Respect

Respect is such a simple word but sometimes people forget its meaning. I think that it is important to treat people as you'd like to be treated and I am often amused about the concern around cultural respect. I think it's simple. It doesn't matter which race you are; if I treat you respectfully, you will give it back to me.

I am not always a traditionalist but I do believe that people should be treated with respect. For me, it's simple. Just be respectful. Use your manners. Everyone responds to that. You've just got to be polite and people will be polite back to you. Be an arsehole, they'll also give it back to you.

What's the point of going in confrontational? If

you and I meet for the first time, our subconscious makes an evaluation of the other. And that happens within one one-hundredth of a second. You might be given information that contradicts your initial feeling, but your brain will help you to forget that. And you'll try to maintain that original impression. According to Stanford University, that original feeling is 99 per cent correct. I was sent to Stanford on a week-long CEO boot camp by Te Ohu Kaimoana, which was created in 2004 out of the Māori Fisheries Settlement between Māori and the Crown. At Stanford they taught us things like the best time to make decisions (in the morning) and how a brain works. It was invaluable.

I've always looked at it from this perspective: if you and I meet for the first time and I'm immediately in your face, for us then to have any form of relationship, we're first going to need to break the barrier down that I created by being immediately in your face. Behaving aggressively like that just doesn't make sense to me. I've always found it far easier just to be upfront.

The people I tried to emulate in treating others with respect were my grandfather, Rangi, and my uncles. Don't go in confrontational because there are always ways around things. And it works. Well, it's worked for me. Other than some of the rows at the table, I don't think I've ever been challenged throughout New Zealand.

Try your best and you will also get respect back.

Back in 1999, we'd just finished a Ngāi Tahu roadshow, which was the tribe's way of reaching out to members of the tribe who did not live in Te Waipounamu, and were in Auckland, when Jono Crofts said, 'You know that the Koroneihana is on.'

'What's that?' I said, not knowing much about it.

'The Māori Queen's coronation ceremony,' he said. 'We can't come to Auckland when that's on without paying our respects.'

So three busloads of us went down to Tūrangawaewae, where the Koroneihana is held, and when we got to the gate of the marae I was told that I was to do the whaikōrero for Ngāi Tahu. This was beginning to feel a lot like that terrifying day at Parliament when we signed the Treaty settlement.

'But I don't speak te reo,' I found myself saying, once again.

'You will be all right, we're behind you,' members

of my tribe said. Well, that was reassuring. I bumbled my way through and forgot how to finish. I just stood there like a bloody stunned mullet and then said, 'The greetings of Ngāi Tahu to Waikato Tainui.' The whole paepae burst out laughing. I was looking for the crack to disappear into, but every man on that paepae said something nice.

If you just stand up and speak in te reo and then English that's okay. The only ones that feel silly about it are us. I was put in my place about that one day by Harry Mikaere from Hauraki. I'd got involved with the Treaty Tribes Coalition over the fisheries settlement and they wanted me to go with them to visit other tribes.

I was reluctant. 'Oh, you know my reo is shit,' I said.

Harry looked at me and said, 'You're a typical bloody Ngāi Tahu. Look, Mark, when we got involved with you, basically Ngāi Tahu had two speakers of te reo. Now, it doesn't matter which Ngāi Tahu marae we go to, there's three or four of your young guys that get up and speak. Yeah, you're not fluent, but all we see is how far you have come. You Ngāi Tahu have got this little thing in your heads that every other tribe in the country speaks te reo but you. You know my elder, Toko? Well, he had to go to classes to learn how to speak Māori. He wasn't brought up in the reo either. Get over yourself.'

You can also win respect by seeking out the right people. At the Treaty Tribes meetings, I used to disappear after the pōwhiri and go straight out the back to see the cooks, because that's where all the real information is. The other chairs from around the country once told me, 'You do more to get things through for us than we can by going out the back talking to the cooks. You come at it without any bias from us and the people listen to you.'

One of the nicest roundabout compliments I ever had was in 2008, when I hosted the Iwi Chairs Forum at Takahanga Marae. Bill English, Georgina te Heuheu and Chris Finlayson were there representing the government and I gave them a talk on the changing demographics of Aotearoa. Aunty Darcy was sitting beside Timi te Heuheu. Not knowing who he was, she said to him, 'That lady MP, what do you think of her?'

'I think she's amazing,' Timi said. 'She's my wife.'

Then Timi went on about me. 'Your nephew's got a pretty rare ability. We've been in meetings with officials and your nephew will just stand up and in three or four sentences explain everything to us, in such a simple manner that everyone gets it. He's got a real skill like that. He can take complicated issues and make them simple. That's why we love dealing with him.'

I just think, why take 10 minutes to state what you should say in three sentences? What is the point of wasting life like that? But, as Uncle Bill had told me, out of anyone's mouth can come a diamond. You've just got to learn how to listen to hear it. Don't judge. It was good advice but hard to follow sometimes.

He mahi kai takata, he
mahi kai hōaka.

It is work that consumes
people, as greenstone
consumes sandstone.

Time

When Ngāi Tahu built the Christchurch City Council headquarters, it was a $113 million deal to make it a Green Star building. Green Star is an internationally recognised rating system for sustainable buildings. We started out at a 6 per cent return. Some property developers told me that they wouldn't get out of bed for that. I thought, Wouldn't you? Have you seen the full deal? It was a great deal.

There are a lot of stories out there about how conservative Māori are. I would argue that we have different time horizons to a lot of companies, which means we have an intergenerational approach and we are risk-averse because we are there for our people. We prefer to do business with entities with similar profiles.

In some shape or form, Te Rūnanga o Ngāi Tahu has got to be here for generations. As the whakataukī says: 'Mō tātou, ā, mō kā uri ā muri ake nei — For us and our children after us'. Who's got the same sort of profile? Iwi, government, local authorities and tertiary institutions — they all have the same time horizons as we do. They are our partners of choice.

Why do I like local government and government? Well, look at the police stations and court buildings that we have bought. I don't care how bad a recession gets, courts and police don't leave their buildings. Nor do councils. So, all through the hard times you've still got a guaranteed cashflow. And if you can do enough of that type of business to cover all of your costs, then everything else you make is cream.

The contribution of iwi to New Zealand Inc. is often underestimated. Here's an example. In 2002, we had a bit of a review of the Ngāi Tahu fishing company. We had a look at what our returns were through selling the fish, what we paid out on wages to the commercial fishers, and which goods and services were provided. Well, back in 2002 our fishing company, which was a third of the size it is today, was delivering $126 million per annum into the South Island economy. Multiply that by three and you get some idea of the contribution Ngāi Tahu is now making to the nation's economy, not to mention the jobs we provide.

The same thing happened in Taranaki. Business and Economic Research Ltd (BERL) was brought in by the Taranaki Regional Council to do an economic review. At random, BERL chose four Taranaki iwi. Those four iwi were actually contributing more than $500 million per annum to the economy in Taranaki, but most local people didn't realise it. Most of Taranaki thought those iwi members were 'dole people' and yet the dole people were and are major contributors to the economy.

I gave a speech one day to the Chamber of Commerce in Wellington about the change in demographics in Māori business. After that meeting, I met the chief executive of Federated Farmers. He wanted to know what I had been doing that day, so I told him.

'I've spoken to the Chamber of Commerce, where I talked about demographics and Māori business,' I said. 'You know, organisations like Te Āti Hou, Parininihi ki Waitotara and Tuaropaki.'

'Who are they, Mark?' he asked.

'You've got to be kidding me,' I said. 'Te Āti Hou have 41,000 acres of operating farms. In total, they own 44,000 acres up in the Whanganui region. PKW is the biggest supplier of milk to Fonterra in the Taranaki region and is worth about $350 million. Tuaropaki is a billion-dollar entity with two thermal power stations and 9000 acres of farms. And there's you, the CEO of Federated Farmers, and you've never heard of them. This is shameful.'

Within three weeks, he had visited the lot and raved about them to me, but was nonplussed that he had never heard of them until I had pointed them out. I said, 'That's the problem then. There's $50 billion worth of Māori business out there and you guys never see it. You never see a thing.'

I have often been asked about the economic success of Ngāi Tahu and what lay behind it. I think we were realistic about risk and we took a long-term view on investment. We also wanted to make sure that we built an economic base for the iwi — and anyway, it was written into our rules. One of the other key reasons is that we always chose the best person for the job, regardless of race. In fact, that is what the tribe told us at an annual meeting shortly before we settled

Te Kerēme with the Crown. When the structure for Te Rūnanga o Ngāi Tahu went through in 1996, we were instructed by the people that we should always take the best for every position. And basically, yes, the tribe would like to see Uncle Joe having the job, but if Uncle Joe doesn't have the skills, then Uncle Joe's not allowed to get the job. I think that's one of the best directions ever given by the tribe.

And, of course, Ngāi Tahu didn't go out and create our own businesses. We went out and bought businesses, and all of those businesses came with staffing regimes already, and the bulk of them were Pākehā. I was asked one time, 'What can you do to increase Māori employment?' I said, 'Well, I could sack all the Pākehā that are working for us, that would give us an extra 400 Māori jobs straight away. But then I think we'd end up in court.'

We had a general philosophy of training young Ngāi Tahu to play their part in taking the tribe forward but to get there, we would always choose the best person for the role, regardless of ethnicity.

Sonny Tau came to visit me when he was chair of Ngāpuhi. I photocopied all the documents relating to our structure. These had a value to Ngāi Tahu Holdings of around $120,000 and here I was giving it — our intellectual property — away for free. But as I explained, if the result was that other iwi would work with us in business then it was more than worth it. The chief executive at the time admitted he hadn't thought of it like that and told me to give away whatever I liked. It was also, I believed, an expression of our values, particularly manaakitanga and whanaungatanga.

I also am a fan of the American thinker Professor W. Edwards Deming, who believed that the man at the top is no more important than the man at the bottom. He reckoned that people should come first, and so do I. We didn't lay anyone off during the global financial crisis because we practised our values. Deming was also largely responsible for the success of Japan's post-war manufacturing boom and his philosophy of co-operation and continual improvement resonates with me. He believed it was more important to avoid blame, and to see mistakes as opportunities to improve.

So are Māori really being so conservative? Show me. The difference is time horizons. It's very different economics to short term. Māori think long term. We were conscious that our tribe had waited a long time for justice and we couldn't let them down. Our people had high expectations, and so did we.

We researched companies that had lasted more than 100 years to find out the cause of that longevity. We also looked at endowment colleges around distribution and chose a model of 4 per cent of the net asset value per annum, so that is what we aim for.

Kīngitanga

I first met the Māori Queen in the late 1990s, when she was in Christchurch and she rang Te Rūnanga o Ngāi Tahu to ask if I'd come to the Park Royal Hotel to meet her. I went over, shaking, to be honest — this was Dame Te Atairangikaahu, the Māori Queen. But within five minutes she had made me feel so relaxed.

Dame Te Ata had her own style. She cared very much how the people were. She was, in many ways, just an ordinary lady, which doesn't sound very royal when I put it like that, but there was something about her. She was lovely to talk to and didn't put on any unnecessary airs or graces.

I had been with her for about an hour when she

invited me to stay for a meal. I said to her, 'On this hand, I've got the hotel food you're offering me; on the other hand, my wife's got a pot of pūhā on. What would you do?'

'I'd go home, dear, if I were you,' she said. 'And if I didn't have all these people with me, I'd come with you.' That's the type of person she was.

Oh, she was clever. She's the person I went to when I came up with the concept of the Iwi Chairs Forum. In 2004, the foreshore and seabed legislation was imposed on Māori. Then National ran its 2005 election campaign with the slogan, 'Kiwi not Iwi'. It was all about getting rid of the Māori seats in Parliament — 'Let's get rid of Māori privilege,' and all that nonsense. Labour only just won that election and my concern was, well, if politicians could ditch Māori rights on the foreshore and seabed, even though the courts came out and found in favour of Māori, they could do the same to the Treaty of Waitangi.

I asked myself the question: If that were to happen, what have the tribes got left? And my answer was, simply: ourselves.

My dream was to do a geographic sweep across the country and to invite, say, 30 iwi chairs to my marae, Takahanga, to discuss a collaborative approach. So, I made an appointment with Dame Te Ata and went to see her. Would she support me? The answer was yes. It seemed to me that every iwi in the country was doing something similar. We were all trying to create social change for our people. That was the whole purpose behind it. It was always said that the Crown was responsible for social change but that didn't mean that we were just going to sit back and let everything be done to us.

When Dame Te Ata said yes, she also gave me a warning. 'I cannot guarantee that all branches of Tainui Waka will turn up. But I most certainly will advocate on your behalf.'

I put out 30 invitations and 36 tribes turned up to the first meeting, including all the branches of Tainui Waka.

The third time I met Dame Te Ata was at our office in Hereford Street, when she came to tono, to ask for pounamu for Tā Robert Mahuta's headstone. At the pōwhiri for her, I said that I knew why she was there; she did not have to ask. We were already out, sourcing the pounamu, and as soon as we found a piece, I would contact Tainui.

When I got the pounamu for the headstone, Nanaia Mahuta and her mother Raiha came down to have a look at it. They both burst out crying when they saw it. Nanaia asked if she could do a karakia, and as she did the whole building was dead still. It was the most powerful karakia I've ever heard.

They wanted to take the pounamu, which weighed about 60 kilograms, back on the plane with them, in a seat of its own.

I said, 'Oh, I don't think Air New Zealand will put this on the plane.' I called the airline. 'Absolutely not,' they said. 'It has to go in the hold.'

Nanaia and her mum reckoned they weren't doing that. 'No, we'll come back down in a truck,' they said. About four days later, they arrived back in Christchurch in a ute. I put the pounamu in the middle seat and they drove back to Ngāruawāhia.

It was jewellery-grade pounamu, thanks to Mawhera Incorporation on the West Coast. The stonemason remarked on it. 'It's one of the best pieces of pounamu I've ever seen,' I was told.

As I normally did, I didn't just take a whole group with me from the South Island to the unveiling. Instead, I went to our whakapapa unit and got some contacts from the north. 'I'm coming up for the unveiling of Tā Robert Mahuta's headstone. If you want to come, meet me at the gateway,' was the message that went out. That way, I incorporated the North Island Ngāi Tahu members. On the day of the unveiling, 36 of them were waiting for me at the gate.

The unveiling was at Hopuhopu, an old military camp north of Ngāruawāhia that had been given to Waikato Tainui in 1988 as part of their Treaty settlement. It was a wickedly hot day, about 30 degrees. As we stood waiting to go on, a young guy approached me and asked, 'Are you Mark Solomon? Te Atairangikaahu wants you and the Ngāi Tahu family to sit with her.'

We were marched across in front of everybody. A group of old women was sitting with Dame Te Ata and this young guy said to them, 'Ladies, get off the seats.'

'No, no, man, I'm not sitting in an elder's seat,' I protested.

'Not your marae,' he said. 'Ladies, get off the seats.'

So all these old ladies sat behind us on the tar-seal in the heat. I was embarrassed, to put it mildly. As I sat down, right behind Dame Te Ata, she turned around and handed me a programme. I was going through it, and when I got to the middle page I must have made a noise because I heard 'unveiling Ngāi Tahu'.

Dame Te Ata turned to me with a big smile on her face and said, 'Mark, I want your kaumātua and your kuia to go up and take the kākahu off the headstone. I want you to go with them and read out the inscription on the stone.'

Kūkupa Tirikātene and Ruruhia Waitere Moke (née Palmer), whose husband George Moke is Tainui and whose son, Tom, was secretary of Tainui Trust Board, were the two Ngāi Tahu elders. They went up and lifted the kākahu off. I read out the inscription, then we went back to our seats and sat down. I saw Nanaia Mahuta roll the kākahu up, then hand it to Bishop Mariu, who was the MC, and he brought it to Dame Te Ata. As he got to her, I heard her say, 'This will do.' She stood up, turned to me and said, 'Ngāi Tahu, mō koutou.' She then handed me the kākahu.

A voice came over the loudspeaker, 'For the next part of the proceedings, Te Atairangikaahu, the Mahuta whānau and Ngāi Tahu only are to go into the Endowed College for the unveiling of the photograph of Sir Robert.'

So we walked across into the college and the

unveiling was done. She said, 'Now, when we go back, Mark, your uncle is to sit on my left and you are to sit on my right on the paepae.' We went and sat down. We were the only men. You've got to be kidding, I thought to myself.

She said, 'I am now going to name my nomination for Kahui Ariki [her representative on Te Arataura] and I want your answer here and now, Tainui, that you support my nomination. I name Raiha Mahuta.'

Te Kauhanganui is the governing council of Waikato Tainui. Its executive board is Te Arataura, which has 10 representatives elected from Te Kauhanganui and an eleventh member appointed by the Māori Queen. Raiha is not Tainui, she is Ngāti Hine, an iwi with a rohe in Northland, but there was no dissent that she would be Te Ata's representative on the governing council of Waikato Tainui. All you could see were Tainui men with their heads down, saying, 'Āe lady, āe lady, āe lady.'

Dame Te Ata then sat down and said, 'Well, it's their turn to talk and I hope they hurry up, I'm hungry.' No one spoke. The whole hui just came single file in front of us. Some stopped and mihied to Tā Robert's headstone. She then turned to me, 'Mark, are you and your whānau coming out to

Waahi?' Waahi was her marae in Huntly.

'Yes,' I said.

'Wait at the gate for me.'

As we were leaving Hopuhopu, a guy came up to me to say, 'I've been sent to tell you the whakapapa of the kākahu. It was made by a woman called Iti Rawiri specifically for the signing of the Tainui settlement. In fact, the documents were laid on it when they were signed. I have been told to tell you it is for wearing not for hanging.' We then went out to Waahi, and we had been there for about half an hour when a car drove in through the crowd and stopped beside us and out hopped Dame Te Ata.

'Apologies for keeping you waiting, Mark,' she said. 'Would you please come to the gate with your whānau.' So the karanga went out, we walked on, there was a paepae, the orators' bench, and Uncle Ku and I turned to peel off.

'No, no, stay with me,' Te Ata said.

Further on, there was another paepae where she sat. Again, we went behind her.

'You two sit on the front,' she said. We were the only two men on that paepae. She turned to me with a big smile and asked, 'Would one of you like to respond on my behalf?'

‘It’ll be Uncle Kūkupa,’ I said. ‘He’d love to.’

Uncle Ku responded on her behalf, then one of the manuhiri spoke, then he turned to the manuhiri pae and said, ‘Tēnei taha. Kau mutu. This side is finished. Just one speaker.’

Now on that marae, at an unveiling, you don’t do the hongi, you only do the harirū. Dame Te Ata introduced me to every person on the paepae individually. And then I peeled off. About half an hour later, Nanaia Mahuta came up to me, ‘Mark, Te Atairangikaahu wants to see you,’ she said.

I went to see her. ‘When the call comes for kai, your uncle is on my left, you’re on my right and you’re to sit at the table with me,’ Dame Te Ata said.

But the call didn’t come until 2 p.m. and I was booked on a 5 p.m. flight back to Christchurch. I went up to Dame Te Ata and said, ‘I know the kawa is that no one can leave the table until you’re finished. So I won’t come in because I’m on a five p.m. flight.’

‘Yes, you will,’ she said. ‘And as soon as you’re ready to leave, just stand up and walk out.’

When I did, the whole hall went dead silent. All eyes were on me as I walked out.

When I got back home that night, I rang Harry Mikaere.

'Harry, I think I know what happened. What do you think happened?' I asked him.

'You've been put up on a pedestal.'

The last time I met Dame Te Ata was at the final Koroneihana before she died. After the pōwhiri, I'd gone round the back to talk to the cooks. About an hour later, Archie Taiaroa, the leader of the Whanganui River iwi, came storming up to me and said, 'Would you get your backside on the paepae? They've been looking for you.'

'No, no. Uncle Ku's there,' I said.

'They want *you*.' He was adamant.

'I hear you've been looking for me,' I said to Dame Te Ata when I got into the wharenui. 'I'm sorry, I've been out the back with your cooks.'

She burst out laughing. 'I told them that. You're either out the back with the cooks or you're out on the road having a smoke. I want you to sit on the mahau when I give my speech.'

In my opinion, it was her goodbye speech. That's what it sounded like when she spoke.

On the day of her tangi, we brought the kākahu back. I said to Uncle Ku, 'Lay it.'

There's a way of laying a kākahu on a casket. A few lay it with the top of the kākahu facing the head — that means bury it. It goes with them. We put the kākahu the opposite way on her casket, which meant that it was not to be buried. We would be taking it back. As soon as we sat down, the two old kuia sitting either side of the casket stood up, picked up the kākahu and turned it round. It was to be buried with her.

A Ngāi Tahu elder wanted to go and have a row with them about it but I said no. 'The honour was that it was given to us and it's appropriate that we bring it back when she dies. And you're not going to demand it. You can't have a row about that.'

What I respected most about Dame Te Ata was her āhua, her nature — just the way she was. She was a beautiful person. And you knew she was important; she had that presence about her, but she was also very gentle. You knew you were standing in front of someone special. For whatever reason, she always treated me really well.

Around 2004, it was announced that Tainui had lost $46 million, but they have recovered nowadays, for sure. I thought I needed to help out, back then. I just rang, made an appointment with the chair and went up to see him. 'I'm just simply here to say whatever my iwi can do to help, we're here,' I said.

When Tainui got into trouble, it became, 'Look at how dumb Māori are.' Tainui got 15 months of public humiliation for losing $46 million.

When Ansett New Zealand lost $60 million, the media hardly even mentioned it. We the taxpayers bailed out Air New Zealand to the tune of $900 million. But Tainui were publicly humiliated for 15 months. That's just the way New Zealand is. It's a racist country.

To give another example. I was invited to an editors' conference. The invitation asked if I would give them a talk on the Ngāi Tahu structure and our aspirations. There was a 'P.S.' on the bottom of the letter: 'If you have issues with the print media, please feel free to raise them.' I certainly did. They got a tirade from me on how they had treated Tainui. I went through the coverage and all the different companies that were in trouble at the same time and the coverage they got, and then said, 'What I don't understand is the different style of reporting.'

Tim Pankhurst, who at the time was the editor of *The Press*, leapt to his feet. 'Because it's called bloody public money,' he said.

I said, 'Oh, yeah? How much public money did Tainui get?'

'They got $170 million,' he said.

'They did not,' I replied. 'They got $170 million worth of value. The bulk of the Tainui settlement was blocks of land, not cash. You say it's public money, but what did you call the bailout of Air New Zealand? Taxpayers paid for that. You didn't humiliate them publicly. Is it different because it's a white man? And while you're on your feet, Mr Pankhurst, is your neighbour Māori or Pākehā?'

'My neighbour's a Pākehā.'

'So if he goes out or she goes out and commits a crime or does something wrong, are you guilty or responsible?'

'Of course I'm not responsible,' he said.

'Then how come when Mike Smith attempts to cut down the tree on One Tree Hill in Auckland, your editorial headline says "Māori". You blame the whole race for the actions of an individual and yet you just acknowledged you wouldn't do that to a white person.'

Rangi and Miriama Solomon née Beaton-Morel. Darcia Solomon Collection, courtesy Ngāi Tahu Archive, 2021-0842

ABOVE Mark with his family at Belfast, Christchurch, in the early 1960s. From back left: Mark's mother, Nyra May, and his father, George; middle: Mark and his brother, Wayne; front: his sisters, Rana and Keri.

BELOW Mark at Belfast School in the early 1960s.

ABOVE Mark some time in the early 1970s.

BELOW Mark and Maria Solomon on their wedding day in 1974.

ABOVE Mark and members of Ngāi Tahu outside Parliament before the Ngāi Tahu Claims Settlement Act was passed in 1998. Te Rūnanga o Ngāi Tahu Collection, Ngāi Tahu Archive, 2017.0261

BELOW Mark in the gallery of Parliament in 1998 as the Ngāi Tahu Claims Settlement Act is passed. To his right is Tā Tipene O'Regan and to his left is Ngāi Tahu kaumātua Edward Ellison. Te Rūnanga o Ngāi Tahu Collection, Ngāi Tahu Archive, 2017.0261

ABOVE Mark and his uncle Bill, Wiremu Solomon, outside Parliament in 1998. Te Rūnanga o Ngāi Tahu Collection, Ngāi Tahu Archive

BELOW Mark with then Minister in Charge of Treaty Negotiations Doug Graham and then Prime Minister Jenny Shipley at Ōnuku Marae for the Crown's formal apology to Ngāi Tahu in November 1998. Courtesy Te Rūnanga o Ngāi Tahu

ABOVE The paepae at Takahanga Marae in Kaikōura in 2013 during the celebrations of Tā Mark's knighthood. Courtesy Tony Bridge

BELOW Ngāi Tahu kaumātua David Higgins MCs during the celebrations at Takahanga Marae. Courtesy Tony Bridge

ABOVE Left: Trevor Howse, 2013. Courtesy Tony Bridge. Right: Darcia Solomon, known to Mark as Aunty Darce, 2013.

BELOW Left: George Tikao, 2013. Right: Kūkupa Tirikātene, 2013. Courtesy Tony Bridge

ABOVE Tā Mark at a media interview at the Ngāi Tahu Hui-a-Iwi in Ōtepoti Dunedin in 2015. Courtesy Te Rūnanga o Ngāi Tahu

BELOW Tā Mark's kākahu is adjusted by Rānui Ngārimu at Takahanga Marae. Courtesy Tony Bridge

I think that challenge did bring a change. *The Press* was very different in its coverage following that. In fact, I remember a *Press* reporter ringing me when we had that taniwha issue in Hamilton, which meant part of a road had to be slightly rerouted. I could hear the giggle in her voice as she asked, 'Mr Solomon, can I interview you about the taniwha issue?'

'Oh, yes, please do,' I said. 'It's absolutely ridiculous. Next they'll be talking about angels, demons and a man that can walk on water.'

There was a chuckle and she said, 'I think I get your point.'

'It's not silly,' I continued. 'It's just different to your belief system. You don't have a right to ridicule it just because it's different to what you think.'

'Good point, Mr Solomon,' the reporter said. 'There won't be an article. Thank you.'

Everything's changing now. When Ngāi Tahu achieved our settlement, the media and sections of the public thought the world was going to come to an end. But later, when Te Tau Ihu, the eight iwi at the top of the South Island, got their settlement, the reaction was, 'Look at this, this will bring $300 million into the economy. This will create jobs.' Everything that was reported was positive. It had been the opposite down here a few years earlier when Ngāi Tahu settled with the Crown.

I think a lot of the opposition was the result of ignorance. I confronted that in the South Island by getting out and talking about the myths of the Treaty process. And the thing that really hit the button when I explained what the settlement was about was when people realised that, actually, the settlements were only about 1–1.5 per cent of the asset base that had been stripped from Māori in the nineteenth century. All they had ever been told was that it was public money and that it was a gravy train for Māori. People are still told that, but there is no gravy train.

If you look at business start-ups, about 50 per cent fail. You look at the Māori record, and I don't care whether they had a capital injection or not, every settlement was a start-up. At Ngāi Tahu, we started with eight staff in 1996 and increased to around 45 just before settlement two years later. It was a gamble, but it worked. And of these start-ups, only about two or three have got into trouble. The performance record is in fact far better than most Pākehā businesses.

Ko te kāhui mauka, tū tonu,
tū tonu, ko te kāhui takata
karo noa, karo noa ka haere.

The people will perish but
the mountains shall remain.

Kotahitanga

My vision for Māori is that we should look at ourselves as a collective and work together economically. To do that, we needed to cherry-pick the assets of the country. The vision of the Iwi Chairs Forum, which meets four times a year, is kotahitanga, which essentially means unity and working together. The forum has established iwi leaders' groups to address particular kaupapa, like fresh water, and to engage directly with iwi and the Crown.

The forum is guided by the whakataukī 'He waka kōtuia kāhore a tukutukua ngā mimira', which means a canoe that is interlaced will not become separated at the bow. In unity there is strength.

I've always promoted the Treaty Tribes model

among iwi. Under that model, you paid your fees based on the length of your coastline. Well, of course Ngāi Tahu is the biggest shareholder — we've got a coastline longer than the whole of the North Island — but then you have a little iwi like Ngāti Tama up in Golden Bay. They paid a fraction of what we did but under the Treaty Tribes model they have exactly the same vote as we do. Just because you pay the biggest amount doesn't mean you get the biggest vote.

I like that, and my way of promoting business is that if you put up 20 per cent of the capital, you get 20 per cent of the profit but you also get to pay 20 per cent of the costs. And the voting is just one iwi, one vote.

The Iwi Chairs Forum was never set up as a decision-making body and I've deliberately argued that it is not a decision-making body. The original purpose was to bring us together to share information so that we could make the best-informed decisions possible. We are there to talk, which wasn't happening in the past. Governments have tried to shunt the forum to the side but I believe its primary purpose is to enable Māori to engage and talk with one another.

Kaiwhakahaere

Weekends as kaiwhakahaere were simple: if you want to deal with your people who, in the main, are a working-class people, you go to them when they've got free time, not the other way around.

I was probably a more insular person before I became kaiwhakahaere. I wasn't a public person at all, ever. Even now, I'm quite happy at home with a book. Before I took on the role I'd never done public speaking in my life. But right from the start I remember thinking that I would treat people the way I'd like to be treated — I suppose you could call it a bit Christian. I would keep things simple and be totally open and transparent.

There's nothing wrong with making mistakes as

long as you learn from them. Mistakes only become an issue when you keep repeating the bloody things. And people will respect you if you own up to mistakes. If I did something and I said, 'Look, I'm sorry. I did this and it's messed up that,' I gained respect. I believe in being upfront with people and they respect that.

What I found among Māori is that you can make a blunder but as long as you're honest about it, people will say, 'Oh, you dickhead, do your job properly. Go and do your job.' But if you try to fudge it, they don't want to know you. And rightfully so.

Around 2003, I said to the contract review committee that I thought the role of kaiwhakahaere had gone up to a new level. When I started, it was a regional role and now it had become a national role. Should I continue or retrench? Continue, they said. Then a couple of years later, I said the role had become international. So I just developed. I could have stumbled anywhere along the way but, thankfully, I didn't. I could not have done the job without my staff. I am a prolific reader, which helped.

Everything is about relationships. It doesn't matter what field you're in, it all comes down to relationships and how you deal with people. There is nothing magical about it. The first row I ever had with the then chief executive of Ngāi Tahu Holdings was over his view that any business or contract had to be screwed right down to the last cent. I argued that it was a dumb way of dealing with people. 'Why would I want to do repeat business with you?' I asked him.

In my whole time as the chair of Te Rūnanga o Ngāi Tahu, I only had one public challenge and that was at Waitangi. I stood up at the Iwi Chairs Forum and said that I was going back to Christchurch that evening because there was going be the first public discussion on water rights the next day at Ōnuku Marae. A guy in the audience stood up and nutted off in Māori at me. I ignored him, and he must have been told off by someone because later he came up to me in the hotel dining room and asked me to explain what I had been saying.

I said, 'Well, I can gather from your kōrero that you nutted off because you've been trying to talk to your local Pākehā council and all they've done is this, this, this, this, this and this.'

'Yes.'

'So, when you go and talk to your council, how do you talk?'

'Whaddya mean?' he said.

I said, 'Well, do you speak aggressively or calmly? How do you expect them to respond to you? You've got to explain what you mean. If you don't explain it to them, you may as well talk to the wall. If you came into a room and everyone was Chinese and they only spoke in Chinese would you understand what they were talking about? It's the same thing. You have to explain it in terms that they understand.'

'How would you explain it?' he asked.

I said, 'Well, when my Uncle Bill went to the Kaikōura council and explained the concept of "ki uta ki tai" or "from the mountains to the sea", it was his way of saying that what we do in the mountains will have a flow-on effect into the lowlands and a flow-on effect into the sea; that nature's holistic, it doesn't have barriers and divisions, that it all flows into each other and you have to look at it in a holistic manner.

'When my uncle finished explaining his concept, the mayor said, "Bill, that's quite beautiful."

'"Good," said Uncle Bill. "Your job is to explain it to the Pākehā community."

'He did, and the philosophy has been adopted by the people of Kaikōura. If you go into my town now, there's an amphitheatre in the middle of the town called "Ki Uta Ki Tai" — from the mountains to the sea.'

People understand a holistic concept of nature — especially in Kaikōura, where the mountains are literally next to the sea — if it is explained in a calm manner. No one responds well to an aggressive approach, especially when they don't understand it.

One time, I was invited to speak to the three tribes of Tauranga: Ngāi Te Rangi, Ngāti Ranginui and Ngāti Pūkenga on Ngāi Te Rangi Marae. A kuia stood up and asked, 'We're all fighting like hell over this Treaty process. Have you got any advice for us?'

I said, 'Well, tāua, why do you say that there's three tribes? Would it be fair to say today that you're all pretty much fully intermarried?'

'Yes.'

'Well, have you ever heard of a concept called whanaungatanga?'

And the kuia looked at me and burst out laughing, then said, 'We have to bring a bloody white-skin Māori from the South Island to remind us of our kaupapa. I'm bloody ashamed.'

I was always clear that when Ngāi Tahu dealt with other iwi, we didn't go in thinking we were the big brother. We are the fifth largest iwi in Aotearoa and seen as commercially astute. Yes, we were making commercial deals but we also needed to treat people with respect. It is something that some people in business for Ngāi Tahu sometimes found hard to learn.

Ngāi Tahu are in business in Auckland now. For example, Ngāi Tahu Property, the New Zealand Super Fund and New Ground Capital invested in Kerepeti, a housing development at Hobsonville. Ngāi Tahu Property has expertise and we shared similar investment horizons. We are already one of the largest players in property in Te Waipounamu and we played a big part in the Christchurch rebuild. Hobsonville was a great entry point into the Auckland market.

But if you look at Auckland from a Māori perspective, there are 19 iwi. When our businesspeople go up there, it is important to be polite and visit them all. Just explain what we are there for. We know, we are meeting the tangata whenua. Whatever we do, do not get involved in the politics up there.

While I was kaiwhakahaere, we went to Sydney

on a roadshow, which we would do annually to stay in touch with Ngāi Tahu members who live outside Te Waipounamu. While I was over there, I got an urgent phone call from work. 'Mark, Ngāti Whātua want to meet you urgently. Can we divert you back to Auckland instead of Christchurch?'

When we landed in Auckland, I went to a meeting with Ngāti Whātua ki Ōrākei, at which they told me that our property guys had only talked to an independent director. 'Oh, and you'd better read this letter, Mark,' they said. 'It was sent to us by mistake.'

Then they handed me a letter which read, 'Mark Solomon, kaiwhakahaere of Te Rūnanga o Ngāi Tahu, has asked Crown negotiator Michael Dreaver to broker a relationship with Ngāti Whātua ki Kaipara and Ngāi Tahu.'

The letter appeared to be from someone at Ngāi Tahu Property and hadn't been referred to me. Michael Dreaver was then the chief Crown negotiator for the Tāmaki Makaurau settlement, known by some as the Crown's hatchet man and by others as the go-to man for Sir Douglas Graham, then the Minister of Treaty Negotiations; it depended in your point of view.

I said to the then chair of Ngāi Tahu Property,

'I don't know who sent this letter but don't put them in the room with me 'cause I'll drop them. What you don't understand, and why I'm angry with this, is that you've used my name without asking me. I have had a full relationship with Ngāti Whātua since 2001. In fact, I'm a director of the seafood company Te Ohu Kaimoana because Ngāti Whātua nominated me. The nomination was seconded by Waikato Tainui, who withdrew their nominee to second my nomination. They don't like Michael Dreaver and now you've mixed our names up so we're going to meet with them. I'll have to formally apologise.'

So we met at Hobsonville Point, at the subdivision we were developing with the New Zealand Super Fund. Uncle Ku did the whaikōrero and then I stood up to formally apologise. The chair of Ngāi Whātua ki Kaipara said, 'Oh, Mark, we know it wasn't you. We have no issue with you. We were a bit pissed off about the Michael Dreaver bit, but we knew it wouldn't be you.'

I said, 'Well, I knew nothing about it until I was shown the letter, but I formally apologise on behalf of Te Rūnanga o Ngāi Tahu for this. And I've brought Barry Bragg, the chair of Ngāi Tahu Property, with me to explain to you what we're doing here.'

Barry gave them an overview of what was happening at Hobsonville. When he was finished, they said, 'You do know, don't you, that we own the eight hectares next door to you to the north? Would you like to do a joint venture with us, too, Ngāi Tahu?'

When that meeting was done, I said to my team, 'I've organised another meeting. We're going to meet Te Kawerau ā Maki, who are the tangata whenua of Waitākere, and you're going to meet their kaumātua and kuia. Their CEO is a man called Te Warena Taua.'

We went to see them, were welcomed, and Te Warena said, 'You do know, don't you, that we own the seven hectares next door to the southern end? Would you like to do a joint venture with us, too, Ngāi Tahu? And, Mark, we're so proud that Ngāi Tahu has come to visit us that we've had this done for you,' and he presented me with a carved whale tooth in a big kauri box.

It's just politeness to make sure you meet the tangata whenua and let them know what you would like to do.

We came out of that meeting and I said to our property people, 'I believe we're looking at a potential venture with Auckland University on a bit of their land.'

‘Yes, Mark.’

‘It’s hilly, isn’t it? Is there any flat land next to it?’

‘Yeah, there’s about a four-hectare block across the street.’

‘I know who owns it, Ngāti Whātua ki Ōrākei. But you said there were no tribal interests in this region. I also believe, because I’ve seen the documents, that Ngāi Tahu Property is working with Ngāti Pāoa [an iwi from Hauraki] to build a marae up here. You do know, don’t you, that within a kilometre there are two other marae? One’s an urban authority marae, urban Māori, but it was formally blessed and opened by Ngāti Whātua ki Ōrākei, recognising that it’s on their land. The other marae, which is just up the road, is a Tūhoe marae, and it’s unique because it’s built on stilts. It’s Tūhoe’s way of acknowledging it’s not their land. Ngāti Whātua ki Ōrākei formally opened and blessed it.’

Ngāi Tahu Property knew none of this, so this is why I said to them: use your manners, go and visit the whole lot. Just introduce yourself, otherwise it’s all about Ngāi Tahu, seen as the big bully boy. When you carry the name of Ngāi Tahu, life is not just about commercial deals — it’s about existing in te ao Māori, the world of Māori.

I always told Ngāi Tahu Holdings, 'If you're outside of our takiwā or region, your first point of call is not the business deal, your first point of call is to the tangata whenua, to the people of that land. And if you're going to be doing business in their area, offer them a joint venture. Nine times out of ten, they'll say no, thank you, but the simple fact that you ask is huge.'

An example of te ao Māori running headlong into commercial reality was when Ngāi Tahu Tourism was offered a deal on the thermal resort Waiotapu, near Rotorua. It was on Ngāti Tahu-Ngāti Whaoa land and Ngāi Tahu Tourism wanted to offer a 50/50 joint venture. I was asked if I knew the leadership of the iwi and whether I could organise a conference call.

I jacked it all up. Representing Ngāti Tahu-Ngāti Whaoa was an old fella by the name of Rawiri Te Whare, who has since passed away. I rang Rawiri and said, 'The chief executive of Ngāi Tahu Tourism wants to talk to you about a tourism venture concerning Waiotapu.'

Rawiri said, 'Boy, that's our Whale Watch,' which

was a reference to the company started by Uncle Bill and others. 'We own the land it sits on but we are not going to renew the lease. We'd really like Ngāi Tahu to pull out.'

'Matua, Ngāi Tahu will pull out immediately,' I said. 'I'll catch you up in the future,' and I hung up.

When I told him the outcome, the chief executive of Tourism told me I had no right to tell Rawiri that, presumably because he thought that I was interfering in Ngāi Tahu Tourism deals. But Tourism carried the name of the tribe and had asked me to use my contacts to set up the conference call.

I said, 'You can go to your board, and they can overrule me, but did you not hear what the man said? They own the land, they are not going to renew the lease; you can go and buy out the lease, but as soon as it's finished, get off. What is the point? Not only will you only have a limited time span there, you'll also destroy all future relationships with Ngāti Tahu-Ngāti Whaoa.'

The board told him, 'Well, do as you're told.'

Ngāti Tahu duly bought it. Three weeks later, I was sitting on a plane leaving Wellington beside Andy West, who had held a lot of high-profile roles. We hadn't met, so he introduced himself. 'Excuse me,' he said. 'Are you Mark Solomon? My god, you blew away Ngāti Tahu and Ngāti Whaoa. I'm one of their directors. They were ready for full war. You should've seen their jaws. I reckon they bounced off the ground. They were ready for a fight but you listened to what they had to say. Mark, I've been told to come and talk to you because Ngāti Tahu owns a full thermal field at Reporoa. Would Ngāi Tahu like to go in a 50/50 joint venture in a thermal power station?'

There's the payback. When it comes to commercial ventures, Māori might have a slightly different view to that of a company with Western values. In this case, it would have been pointless to pursue what looked at first glance like a commercial opportunity because we would have ultimately lost, and angered Ngāti Tahu-Ngāti Whaoa.

Another example. Ngāi Tahu Holdings came to me and said they had been offered a potential joint venture with the New Zealand Super Fund and Tauranga City Council to build a huge complex. They wanted me to organise a meeting with the tribes of Tauranga to offer a joint venture. I met one of the Tauranga iwi chairs in Blenheim at the Iwi Chairs Forum. 'Mark, would Ngāi Tahu work with us?' he asked.

'Of course we will. Why?'

‘Well, you know, we’ve all got settlements or are getting settlements, but we’re small players and there are huge opportunities in our rohe, and we wanted to know whether Ngāi Tahu would like to partner with us.’

‘Isn’t this interesting,’ I said. ‘I was actually going to come and talk to you about this today. Our lot want to come and talk to you. So there’s a potential venture, it’s still not quantified yet, but our lot would like to know whether you’d be interested to come in with us.’

My argument in part for creating the Iwi Chairs Forum is that the synergies across the tribes are huge. The opportunities collectively are huge. We’ve just got to get over ourselves and learn to work together.

I found the politics much harder than the business world when I was kaiwhakahaere of Ngāi Tahu. Most politics is not about the issue — most politics is to play the person. If it were strictly about the business, politics would be good because then you’d end up getting a better answer in the end. I came to a pretty quick conclusion that every community has good people and bad people, whiners and the non-whiners. You have the shit-stirrers and the non-shit-stirrers. It's a community and you've got to work within that. And there will always be the doomsayers.

The people of Ngāi Tahu were the highlight of my time as kaiwhakahaere. We had our fair share of scraps around the table, but I loved getting out among the people and into the community. There's bad stuff out there, everyone knows that, but everywhere I went, people were striving to go forward. No one was sitting there living in their doom and gloom and thinking that the world was coming to an end. People were just trying to go forward. And all I saw was the beauty of it.

When we asked the iwi at a series of hui after the settlement what they wanted us to focus on they said the language, the culture and education. They wanted us to look at social issues but they did not want us to become a brown department of social welfare. They wanted us to give a hand up, not a hand out. I came back from those hui absolutely bouncing.

I'm really proud of Whai Rawa, which is the Ngāi Tahu-matched savings scheme that predated KiwiSaver. It has introduced a savings ethic to our people. I grew up in the generation where we were sent to school once a week with our Post Office Savings Bank savings books. We'd have two bob or, if Dad had had a good week driving the taxi, half a crown each to bank. It was just something you did every week. But another one and a half generations later, many have never learnt how to bank. So I was pretty chuffed with the concept of Whai Rawa.

The majority of the money that's been saved has been saved by the kids. Regardless of whether mum and dad put the money in, the bulk of the savings are with the kids. I see that as a real success. It also opened my eyes. Financial literacy programmes were part of Whai Rawa. I went to one where an Irish woman taking the programme started talking about mortgages, about how you can negotiate with the bank. An older woman in the audience said, 'No, dear, when you go into the bank the mortgage rate's up on a board.'

'Yes, but all banks will negotiate and even if you can get a one per cent discount, over a thirty-year mortgage, that's a lot of money,' said the tutor. In that room of 70 people, I was the only one who knew that you could negotiate with a bank. Just something as simple as that will make a difference.

The idea of a Ngāi Tahu business registry will also make a difference. I once got a quote to do up our kitchen and bathroom. The first quote was for $30,000. So I rang Te Rūnanga o Ngāi Tahu and asked, 'Hey, when you register people, do you register their trade or occupation?'

'Why?' the person replied.

'Well, I just got quoted $30,000 on a kitchen and bathroom, and I'd rather give that to a Ngāi Tahu tradie and build the Māori economy.'

There are now around 380 companies on the Ngāi Tahu register, which seems to me to be a really practical and good way of adding to the tribal economy. I imagine everyone will work out who the good ones and the bad ones are. And the tribe will know within a day or two through the kūmara vine if you've messed them around. But what a neat and simple way of building a tribal economy.

The last Iwi Chairs Forum I attended was in Blenheim and hosted by all the tribes of the south. At the formal reception, the three mayors of the region welcomed the iwi chairs and I was asked to respond. I got up after their welcome and thanked them. I asked the South Islanders to step to the right. 'You know, the brown people standing in the hall represent around $2.4 billion worth of assets. Do you want to work with us?' I asked.

'Yes,' they said. 'Of course. It's a no-brainer.'

Earthquakes

I had just come out of hospital after knee surgery when the September 2010 earthquake struck. The noise of it coming woke Maria and me up.

'Is that a train?' Maria asked.

'No,' I said. 'Hang on.'

Bang, and it hit us. As bad as it was, we had no damage at all. Two glasses vibrated off the pantry shelf and broke, and the 42-inch TV crashed onto the dog basket. It broke the dog basket but not the TV.

Maria leapt out of bed while it was still rocking to get to the kids. By the time it had stopped shaking, the quake had thrown the top cupboards of the wardrobe open and dumped all the books onto the new knee I had had done four days earlier.

What sympathy did I get? None. 'I told you ages ago to get rid of those bloody books,' Maria said when she came back into the room.

The February earthquake was a lot different, especially at work. The first one in September didn't take out our computers. Everything was still operating, phones were still going. The second one took out everything. We lost all of our servers. We had to move out of our headquarters in the CBD. Our phone and internet provider, 2degrees, was a huge help. They turned up at Wigram, where luckily Ngāi Tahu had property, and we were able to set up almost straight away with two cartons of cell phones, chargers and batteries all charged. They kept our comms going with the delivery of all those cell phones.

I was in a meeting in a restaurant in Wellington at the time of the quake. There was a TV screen on the wall in front of me. The sound was off but I could see the words running across the bottom. 'Massive earthquake hits Canterbury. Multiple deaths.'

I couldn't ring home, the phones were down. All planes were cancelled. So a group of us met up, went down to the wharf and walked onto a ferry. No one asked us for a ticket. As we were coming into the Marlborough Sounds, I got on my phone and rang my brother John, who was in Blenheim.

'What are you doing, bro?' I asked him.

'I'm just going to bed,' he says.

'No, you're not. You're coming to Picton to pick us up. There's four of us. We want to go home.'

He collected us off the boat and drove us back to Christchurch. We got to Christchurch at about three in the morning. It was dead silent. The first sign of the earthquake I saw was the forecourt of the Belfast Shell garage, which had collapsed.

By about 2 p.m. that afternoon I had organised a meeting with all the tribal groups of Canterbury at Rehua Marae in Ōtautahi. The first person to speak stood up and demanded money from Te Puni Kōkiri for a new subdivision. The second speaker stood up and demanded money for a water system at Rāpaki. The third person who stood up demanded money for his private company. None of these demands had anything to do with earthquake damage. The fourth person to stand up was a woman of about four-foot-nothing who looked at these three and said, 'You dirty, grubby little people. We have just had a massive earthquake. There could be hundreds dead and you're sitting here with your hands out for money.'

Before they could respond, Norm Dewes, who was chief executive of Te Rūnanga o Ngā Maata Waka, stood up and said, 'Hey, Mark. No "me", no "you", mate. Just "us".' That's as simple as it was. Everything went through Ngāi Tahu.

Norm is Ngāti Kahungunu and Te Rūnanga o Ngā Maata Waka is the urban Māori authority in Canterbury. Norm came to Christchurch in the late 1950s under the Māori Trades Training Scheme and worked as a union secretary for 27 years before he got involved with Ngā Maata Waka.

There was a lot of talk at that first meeting about whakapapa but I pointed out that this was about helping *everyone*. About manaaki, which is supporting everyone.

We said, 'Okay, everyone go home. Go and do a stocktake. Think about what you can actually do because we all are victims, too, then get back here tonight at seven with some ideas about how we can help.'

It was agreed that everything would run through Ngāi Tahu and that we would take on all the documentation. I asked, 'Can we adopt Pākehā?', meaning whomever we come across is whom we help. It's not about just working with Māori. That was unanimously agreed to. Actually, I proposed the approach 'Arohanui ki te tangata', which means love for everyone, be adopted.

Another thing I asked was: 'What about our new citizens? The migrants? Like us, they're at the bottom of the ladder and, like us, they're likely to be left out.' Yep, everyone reckoned we should bring them on board.

To me, an earthquake, as scary as it is — and it is bloody scary — is ultimately a natural process of the planet. We drew the short straw this time. It could have been anywhere in the world. But it was terrifying, I don't deny that. I saw both ends of the scale. During one meeting afterwards, a truck went past and there was a vibration. An elderly Māori lady just curled up into a foetal ball, screaming because she thought it was another earthquake. My two moko were in my lounge one day when a little earthquake struck. The seven-year-old stopped and said to her four-year-old sister, 'Oh, it's only about a 3.6. There will be no liquefaction. Come on.' Then I got a lecture from them. 'Don't be scared,' they told me. 'If it's really big, get on the ground.'

I did realise, straight out, that we had to get in touch with our people. And getting that contact was the big thing. People will follow someone who leads, who makes decisions. For quite some time now, I've been out among the different marae across the country talking about Māori resilience in the aftermath of an earthquake or a disaster. What do you do? The reality is we know what to do.

For example, after a disaster, people will turn up at a marae for support or somewhere to stay but they've forgotten all of their medications. So, you need a relationship with the chemist and the doctor. A lot of people's medication has to be kept chilled. What happens when there's no power?

'Oh, I know what to do then, dear,' one kuia said. 'We'll take it to the spring down the back of the marae. It's like an icebox.'

I've spent the last 10 years challenging the control processes of Civil Defence because, while I understand their rationale, what they do is come in, put their authority across everything, and do not work with the local community. Just look at Ōtautahi. We had the student army, we had the farming army, we had all the wardens. These are huge resources that were on the ground but often overlooked by Civil Defence. After the Kaikōura earthquake, in 2016, Red Cross took responsibility for checking out the Awatere Valley, north of Kaikōura. They came back and reported that everything was hunky dory but, in fact, they were missing 14 families because they didn't know the lie of the land and they didn't speak to the locals.

A week after the Kaikōura earthquake, I was invited by iwi to a hui with seven Crown agencies and Civil Defence to talk about what Ōtautahi was like after the earthquake and what the issues were. I talked about the silly little things that had gone wrong, like how the residents of Aranui wanted to stone the army because all they did was go round and round and round in circles blowing up liquefaction and raw sewage as it dried out. It drove the locals down there crazy. Like how there was the nonsense of Civil Defence on one side of the street and Red Cross on the other. They'd get to the end of the street and swap sides and go back the other way, both asking the same questions.

In the first few days after a disaster, it's a matter of

getting things in place. What is our response? How are we going to look after the people who are out there responding?

There were some beautiful stories. Three nights after the quake, I was talking to a Māori nurse who had been out in the community that day. She told me how when she knocked on one door it was opened by a skinhead with a swastika tattooed on his forehead. He looked at the nurse and said, 'Lady, you better come inside.' In the lounge she found the skinhead's elderly, wheelchair-bound Māori neighbour, who was wearing a colostomy bag. The skinhead and his mates had looked after him well and had even changed the bag. This nurse said to me, 'Only in the South Island do you get the skinheads looking after the coloured people.'

I said, 'No. I think they are victims, too.'

I heard about an elderly Pākehā lady in east Christchurch who opened her curtains one morning to see a group of young Māori and Pasifika boys shovelling liquefaction off her lawn. That changed her views.

It's about people. At their heart, people care about others.

There was also plenty of stupidity after the

Ōtautahi earthquakes. On the Friday after the February earthquake we had a meeting at Te Rūnanga o Ngāi Tahu CEO Anake Goodall's house in Westmorland, which is a hilly suburb in the south of the city. Westmorland hadn't sustained much damage at all, but at the bottom of Westmorland Hill there were 30 portaloos all lined up. They stayed there for over three weeks while the eastern suburbs had none.

And then when they did bring the portaloos into the eastern suburbs, there was more stupidity. They went to unload a portaloo and a neighbour said, 'Hey man, can you put it five doors up, please? The couple up there are in their nineties. Put it outside their place.'

And the driver said, 'I'm told to put it here. This is where it's going.'

The earthquake had knocked out a lot of the city's infrastructure and people were without water, sewerage and power, and the mayor, Bob Parker, couldn't understand how people got so upset about the water tankers. The reason was pretty simple, actually. In one incident, it was advertised on radio that a water tanker would be in such-and-such a street at 10 in the morning. People were lining up from 9 a.m. but the truck didn't get there until 3 p.m. All these stressed people and the truck comes five hours late. What did he think was going to happen?

A couple of days after the earthquake, Parker said on radio, 'Look, if you can get out of Christchurch for a while, get out.' Fine, but it meant that every house then had to be searched because what he didn't say was that if you are going to leave, you need to register with Civil Defence so there was a list of houses that had been left vacant.

It is really important in the aftermath of a disaster to know the whereabouts of people. At Ngāi Tahu, we put out a message across all the Māori of New Zealand. Have you got Canterbury refugees with you? If you have, can you ask them this list of questions? Are all the family there? Have you left anyone at home? Et cetera. Then we could feed that into the system.

So how did I access the system? Through knowing people. Connections. It was day eight before Ngāi Tahu got to meet with Civil Defence and that was through King Tūheitia.

'Why don't we have this information about what is available and who is here?' they asked. 'Because we can't get in the door,' I said. It wasn't that anyone resisted but even so, you had to go through about ten people to get to the art gallery, which was the temporary Civil Defence headquarters. Then you had to go through about twenty people to find someone to talk to, and that person invariably couldn't make a decision. It was a totally pointless exercise. Once they saw the data we had, it got us in there and we could start to work. We were part of Civil Defence briefings every morning. It was simple stuff about who was available to help, that sort of thing. Civil Defence seems to assume it has all the answers when often it pays to speak to people with local knowledge.

The other part of my challenge to Civil Defence is about their need for protocol. The Edgecumbe floods of 2017 were a classic example. They cordoned it off. They'd gone through the town and had said everything was hunky dory, but a man turned up at the cordon and said, 'My mother's in there in a wheelchair.'

'No, there's no one there,' they told him.

'My mother's in there,' he said. 'I'm talking to her now on my phone.'

'No,' they said, and refused to let him through. So his mate got a tractor and trailer and they crashed through the barriers.

It takes a long time to get in the door. And usually, around week three of a disaster, you hear a statement from the prime minister about how well Māori organisations have stepped up and are delivering food and so on. A month later, it's all forgotten. They never continue their advantage of a collaborative approach.

Māori can organise; we can reach our communities. But we're only part of it. Local people know the lie of the land. They know what's happened. The simple reality after the Kaikōura earthquake is that when the sun came up, the two car parks of the marae were full because that's where everyone gravitated to.

There was stuff in the media about how we were feeding tourists crayfish and fish after the Kaikōura earthquake. But let's be practical. We had 1500 crayfish in tanks at the Kaikōura fish-receiving depot and the power had gone out. What's the choice? You've got no transport; you can't get in and out of Kaikōura. So Māori helped supply the crayfish and fish through the fishing company.

In the weeks after the February 2011 earthquake,

Ngāi Tahu definitely had more presence in the city. It's funny how things work. Ever since I became kaiwhakahaere, I have had a good relationship with the mayor, but the iwi historically had a terrible relationship at management level. After the earthquakes, the iwi became a statutory partner with CERA (Canterbury Earthquake Recovery Authority; now Ōtākaro Ltd) and began working closely with Christchurch City Council. The earthquakes were a tragedy but they also led to a strong Treaty relationship for Ngāi Tahu. The earthquakes gave us a unique opportunity to design a cityscape that acknowledges our shared past with our colonisers, our shared experiences, and our common future, which certainly wasn't there beforehand.

At a consultation weekend about the future of the city one weekend, 33,000 people were surveyed and 76 per cent said that any new developments should reflect both cultures. That's progress.

I always argue that our responsibility as Ngāi Tahu was to get out and sell ourselves, to show that we're not a threat. We're a proactive part of the community. We *are* the community. Take away the threat. And it's what I've said before: if you and I meet for the first time and I'm immediately in your face, then the first thing you do subconsciously is create a barrier and for either of us to have a relationship, we've then got to waste time breaking that barrier down.

Leadership is just common sense, and it came in handy after the earthquakes. I always had an issue with anyone who tried to force me to have a closed-door policy. Te Rūnanga o Ngāi Tahu is an organisation owned by the people. If I'm available and a Ngāi Tahu person comes and wants to talk to me, let them in.

And when I say leadership is common sense, I also mean that you have to know when to make decisions, when to listen to people. It's about people management.

People were looking for leadership after the earthquakes and I was happy to be a leader. My leadership style was the same as it has always been: no-nonsense but non-confrontational.

Knighthood

When you get a letter offering you a knighthood, all the letter says is that you've been nominated. It doesn't tell you who nominates you. When I got that letter in 2012, Maria and I had a discussion, and we decided we'd turn it down because . . . well, I wasn't that happy about getting a knighthood. It wasn't something I aspired to and we both thought it wasn't us.

And then I made a fatal mistake of speaking about it in front of Aunty Darce. All I got from her was, 'So if you were still working in the foundry, do you think you would've been offered a knighthood?'

'Probably not,' I said.

'So then it must be because of your work you've done with Ngāi Tahu?'

'Possibly.'

'Then who the hell are you to say no? This isn't about you. It's about Ngāi Tahu, and you will accept it.'

She was right and I said so. I accepted because of Aunty Darce.

The official title is a Knight Companion of the New Zealand Order of Merit, for services to Māori and business. I wouldn't have got it as a foundry worker, as Aunty Darce had said.

And after I became Tā Mark, I was shocked at how a whole new set of doors opened, doors that had never been opened before. All of a sudden, I was getting invitations to things that I'd never been invited to before. That's what a knighthood does.

I was only allowed six people at Government House on the day of the ceremony in 2013, so I invited Robyn Walsh to represent Nicky Walsh, who had been my first personal assistant and a huge help to me. And Maria and my three boys went with me, and my sister.

It was a great honour to go to Government House and receive a knighthood, and an even greater honour to be recognised later by Ngāi Tahu at Takahanga Marae, but I still feel a little embarrassed when someone calls me 'Sir' or 'Tā' Mark.

He Toki

He Toki ki te Rika, which is a modern version of Māori trades training, backed by Ngāi Tahu, started after the February 2011 earthquake. When I was interviewed on television on the Thursday after the earthquake, I said that if we didn't use the aftermath of the earthquake to recreate trades training in Ōtautahi, then the whole nation was remiss. The following week in Parliament the issue was raised by Rahui Katene. Paula Bennett, who was then the Minister for Social Development, responded, 'We heard what Mark Solomon said and we are going to start up trades training in Christchurch.' That's how He Toki came about; I just made a throwaway statement. Well, it was fair.

In the 1950s, 1960s and 1970s, Māori trades training provided a first step into trades qualifications for hundreds of young Māori and, as many have acknowledged, was often a first step into friendships and careers. In those years we had hundreds of Māori come here to Ōtautahi for trades training. They often stayed at Rehua Marae, the urban marae in Christchurch, and stayed on in the city.

The recovery was a chance to replicate that. Straight away, as part of the recovery, we were talking of having to bring in thousands of people from overseas, but why do that when we had people here who could be taught?

He Toki ki te Rika was launched by Te Rūnanga o Ngāi Tahu and Canterbury Polytechnic, which is now Ara. I was the founding patron and one of its biggest supporters. We began with a one-year pre-trade training course and later launched an apprenticeship pathway and a leadership pathway. I felt that it was important to support whānau.

Initially, an Industry Training Organisation (ITO) was involved, and about halfway through their course the students in the first cohort held a barbecue. The head of the ITO came down, looked at them and said, 'Never to be employed, never to be employed.'

Half of them, according to him, would never get a job.

'Look at the way they're wearing their caps,' he said. 'They're wearing them sideways.'

That makes them unemployable, right?

He was fired.

After that, we signed a memorandum of understanding with Hawkins construction. What I liked about Hawkins is that they were in the industry and a good number of their employees had come through the old trades-training programme, the Māori one. When they came to talk to the trainees, they brought those original trades trainees, who are now site managers and quantity surveyors. They know the language; they know how to talk to the kids. They know every challenge that an apprentice can go through and are quite free in telling you about it. It was just amazing.

When I started He Toki, there were 789 unemployed Māori in Canterbury. By the end of the first four years of He Toki, that had dropped to 76 so we knew it was making a difference. To date, we have put over 1400 trainees through the programme.

I saw things that really stunned me. One time, a young woman in her twenties stood up and said she was the first in her whānau to get a qualification. 'Awesome,' I said. 'What did you get?'

'I've got my learner's licence,' she replied.

Another young man stood up. 'Matua, if I'm honest, all I've done since I got kicked out of school at fourteen is sit on the couch,' he said. 'I'm on this course because my mate here nagged me that I had to get off my backside and do something. But, matua, do you know what I found out on this programme?'

'What would that be, lad?' I asked.

'That I'm not dumb,' he said.

'What do you mean by that?'

'Well, all I ever got told at school is, "You're dumb, you're dumb, you're dumb," and I believed them. But, matua, on this course we have a test every week. I've had no special tutoring. I've passed every test. I don't mean I've got fifty or fifty-one. I've passed in the seventies in every test. So that's what I've learnt, matua. I'm not dumb.'

I said, 'Well, lad, you don't let anyone tell you you're dumb. You'll have knowledge in your head that they don't have in theirs, does that make them dumb? You can be whatever you want. All you've got to do is apply yourself. Our job is to put the resources behind you to help you get there.'

That young man is now a fully qualified carpenter working for Hawkins in Auckland.

One day, I stopped a kid on the street. I didn't know him, but I recognised his features. 'You're from Tuahiwi?' I asked.

'Yep,' he said.

'What are you doing out on the street? It's a school day.'

'No, I'm a street kid,' he said.

I said, 'No, you're not. Come with me.'

'Where?'

'I'm signing you up to the trades-training programme.'

Today he is a fully qualified carpenter. Every kid has a pathway. We've just got to find the right way to get them on their path.

All the kids had to undergo a drug test. One of the things I made clear upfront was that if they tested positive, they wouldn't be kicked off the programme. We would start another process: how to get them off drugs.

People say He Toki was common sense, but common sense is often a lot of little things, day in and day out, which is probably part of my leadership style. I am a great believer in common sense. I think my simple way of looking at things is about 'us'. Any responses are about 'us'. Everything we get involved in as humans ultimately comes down to the battle between the 'I' and the 'we'. I take a 'we' approach, which means 'we the people'.

In traditional Māori society, you had the rangatira, the chiefs, but in every field you had experts. In traditional Māori culture, it wasn't the right of the ariki or the rangatira or the tohunga to dictate to the experts on how they did their job. A good leader puts his best foot forward. When you're going into battle, you don't have your worst warrior out the front leading — you have your best. When you're going onto the paepae, you put your best speakers up there.

There are two stories that belong to the heritage of this nation, and for a long time only one of those had dominated here in Ōtautahi. After the quakes, we realised what we can achieve when we share a common experience and belief. I was praised for my leadership after the quakes, and I've often spoken about leadership. To me, it's about empowering our people — allowing them the space to identify their own needs and the time to come up with their own ways of addressing those needs and improving their lives.

I've often said that to survive in today's fast-paced world, Māori and the wider community need to consider a much broader range of ideas about leadership. It is always evolving and it's vital that all iwi work with their young people to ensure our national kete is filled with future leadership talent. Our economy and the social fabric of our nation depends on it.

Leadership can be learnt and developed through experience. I am an example of that. I wasn't born into leadership. I had to learn to be a leader as an adult and, in doing so, I often looked back to my uncles and my grandfather — the men I turned to after my father passed away. They have had a profound influence on my life. They have shown me through example that leadership is all about whānau first. Good leadership is inclusive. Always.

Health

When I left Te Rūnanga o Ngāi Tahu, I started with the Canterbury District Health Board (CDHB) as deputy chair. I was a Crown appointee. What was exciting about going on the CDHB was that it had a $1.8 billion budget. I just wanted to be involved in something on that kind of scale, but it turned out to be nothing like I expected.

It was obvious at the first meeting that not only was there trouble at the board but there was also a war going on between the Ministry of Health and the DHB. I became acting chair after the chair was stood down. The board itself was, and is, riven by personalities and politics. About an hour into my first board meeting, I burst out laughing. I couldn't help myself. The chairman said, 'Are you all right, Sir Mark?' I said it was obvious this was a board divided by factions. We'd just had a talk about someone leaking to the media and I felt like I was still working with Ngāi Tahu because the factionalism and the leaks to media were common to both boards, in my experience.

And the nonsense that came through from the ministry just blew me away. For example, as one of three new appointees, I went to Wellington for a new board member induction day. While we were there, the three of us from Canterbury were invited to tour the Ministry of Health. We were subjected to a massive dump about how terrible David Meates, who was then the CEO, and his management were.

At the CDHB, we were dealing with the aftermath of the earthquakes, which had caused a lot of trauma in the community. There's lots of data around trauma and disasters. One statistic, for example, is that 4 to 5 per cent of the population will end up with long-term mental-health issues. A lot more will end up with short-term mental-health issues because of post-traumatic stress syndrome. You don't actually have to have been part of the disaster to get the syndrome.

It all follows a similar pattern. You have a disaster

and within six weeks there's a massive increase in heart attacks and strokes. That goes on for a couple of months. Then it levels off, you have a big spike of mental-health issues, then it'll plateau. Then in year five — whoosh! — it goes off again and starts to manifest. When it comes to children, you can actually see the groupings that are the most affected.

Those who were in the womb at the time can be affected and we won't see the results until a few years later. Those transitioning into kindergarten, those transitioning for the first time into primary school, into intermediate, into high school . . . they are the biggest affected grouping of all children, and that's replicated worldwide after a disaster.

The government has known this, and they knew this straight after the earthquakes. So in 2019 when the Director-General of Health, Dr Ashley Bloomfield, came down to Christchurch, I asked him four questions.

'Ashley,' I said. 'I've got four questions and I want a yes or no answer only, please. Do you accept at this point in time that Canterbury District Health Board has the highest levels of mental-health issues in the country to deal with?'

'Yes,' he said.

'Do you accept that we've just had an influx of Syrian refugees into Christchurch with their own mental-health issues?

'Do you accept that we've just been informed that we will be in charge of hundreds of prisoners with the mental-health issues that go with prisons?

'Do you accept that we've just been informed we're getting four plane loads of Afghani refugees from their war with their mental-health issues?'

He answered yes to my remaining questions, so then I asked him to explain why Canterbury is the second-lowest-funded district health board in the country for mental health, despite the Crown and the Ministry of Health knowing all of this was coming, given the international literature on post-disaster mental healthcare.

He couldn't answer the question. And a year later, I was still waiting for the answer. But that is the reality: Canterbury was and is the second-lowest-funded DHB for mental health in the country. The systems are so inflexible that they can't step in to help in a disaster.

The CDHB announced a $180 million deficit in 2020 (the government has now announced it will wipe the whole deficit). But if you take off the depreciation and the capital charge over the new buildings and the cost of hiring theatres and buildings, the deficit is around $48 million. Operationally, we were in the black. I've argued with Treasury officials about our deficit levels and it amazes me that they have not, as I see it, been able to grasp that if we've demolished 42 buildings and are rebuilding multiple others, plus installing new plant, then that would have a bearing on why our depreciation rates are higher than the other DHBs.

The ministry has called me incompetent, inefficient and totally captured by management, but I am astonished by what has been achieved in Canterbury through innovation and smart thinking. Delivering health is not cheap, yet Cantabrians are getting a modern health system, despite the bureaucratic war going on.

As one example of innovative thinking, Māori were twice as likely not to turn up for appointments at Christchurch Hospital until we introduced a texting process a week before the appointment to remind them. It seems obvious in hindsight but it has worked well. You've got to look at it through the eyes of people who are on the minimum wage. They have to take four hours off work to come into the hospital, find a park and get a test. In many cases, that is the difference between a meal on the table that night and no meal.

Because of our lack of funding, we treated 35,000 elderly in their own homes, as opposed to bringing them into the hospital. We found that they healed better and there was a decrease in repeat presentations, which is a great outcome. It cost us $5 million but saved $24 million in hospital costs.

Health is a huge, complex issue and in New Zealand we are running the infrastructure of a country based on the population of a small city. Given that, we do an incredibly good job. But things are stretched, and they will always be stretched. And as we get older as a population, the cost of healthcare just goes up, and up, and up, and up. The percentage of GDP that New Zealand spends on health is half that of similar nations. We're not even close to Australia's percentage but, despite that, we do some pretty awesome work.

I'm absolutely blown away by what the management and the hospital system of Canterbury managed to maintain post-earthquake, and how they've had to innovate and change the way they're doing things, despite being completely underfunded. They have done an amazing job. I loved being involved. But it's a dirty-dog place to work. I've never worked in an atmosphere like it. It's fair to say that the CDHB continues to face many challenges. Among them is the board's relationship with the Crown. Since I have left, it only seems to have become worse, with the resignation of the CEO and many of the senior management team.

Te Pūtahitanga

I chair Te Pūtahitanga o Te Waipounamu, which is the Whānau Ora commissioning agent for Te Waipounamu and its nine iwi.

It started while I was still kaiwhakahaere of Ngāi Tahu, when Dame Tariana Turia held a consultation hui to promote Whānau Ora at Ngā Hau e Whā Marae, in the eastern suburbs of Ōtautahi. It is not a Ngāi Tahu marae; it is a national marae for everyone.

Turia was then the minister responsible for Whānau Ora and she had convinced the Cabinet that the usual ways of delivering social and health services weren't working for Māori. Whānau Ora was set up in 2010 in response, designed as a whānau-centred approach to delivering well-being and development.

At the hui, I stood up and said, 'Tari, if I can get the other eight tribes of the South Island to work with Ngāi Tahu, could we put a bid in for the commissioning agency?'

'Of course,' she said and laughed. 'If you think you can get the tribes together.'

It took two meetings. I then led the bid to Parliament, where we went in front of a committee and won the right to become the commissioning agency. My only input other than going and putting the bid in was to front up to the politicians. In one meeting, the then Minister for Whānau Ora said, 'I want the commissioning agency to concentrate on the poor.'

I asked him to define 'poor'. Did he mean economically poor, educationally poor or health poor? Poor is a very broad term. What were we talking about?

'Well, you know, Mark,' he said.

I said, 'No, that's why I'm asking you, minister.'

'Well, we're giving you this huge amount of money.'

'Oh, come on, minister. With all due respect, you're giving us chump change. The amount you're paying out is $5 million per annum for the next three years. There are 110,000 Māori in the South Island, so that equates to about $45 each. What do you expect us to achieve with that? What I like about Te Pūtahitanga is that it gives us three years to show that we can deliver programmes in a cost-effective way. But at the end of those three years, minister, I expect a dramatic increase in funding.'

We're up to about $24 million in business-as-usual funding and $12 million in funding for our Covid response. Our parent body is Te Taumata, which is made up of representatives from the nine iwi of Te Waipounamu: Ngāti Apa, Rangitāne, Ngāti Koata, Ngāti Tama ki Te Tau Ihu, Ngāti Toa Rangatira, Te Atiawa, Ngāti Kuia, Ngāti Rārua and Ngāi Tahu. The first eight tribes make up Te Tau Ihu, the iwi at the top of Te Waipounamu, the tangata whenua of that region. Ngāi Tahu is the ninth tribe.

Te Taumata, in a sense, gives us a letter of expectation at the start of the financial year to which we have to respond. There's a core set of values that we operate under. When it comes to the programming, we have the assessments done by an independent body. They say whether it falls under the Whānau Ora criteria and then we award the funding.

We've funded 350 projects so far and they are

whānau-based. The key to Whānau Ora is in local solutions. We envisaged that change can and will come from the flax roots and that the pathway of change to greater self-determination and choice will be created by whānau entrepreneurs and leaders operating on the ground, prepared to take their wider communities with them. We weren't bidding to be the government's alternative welfare net; we were bidding to be an impact investor.

I think Whānau Ora's doing pretty well. We've had some successes; we've had some failures. Some of the funding applications you would never expect. For example, one family got in touch and wanted a navigator — which is what we call staff who are enablers for whānau — because they wanted to paint their fence.

'We're the roughest house in the street,' they said. So through the navigator, they organised the paint, they organised Whānau Ora, and they painted the fence. And then a whole raft of other things came through that they wanted to do, which were all mana-enhancing for the family. Well, I'll call that a massive success. And everything we do, we have independent research done on it so we know whether or not it works.

Forests

The Māori Carbon Collective, which used to be known as the Māori Carbon Foundation, is a commercial entity I joined after finishing as kaiwhakahaere. Carbon farming has paused at the moment, but it offers a great deal for what has been seen as marginal land, usually with multiple owners. That is usually Māori land.

It came about when Dame Tariana Turia and I were invited to meet and advise New Zealand Carbon Farming, a company set up to trade carbon credits, on how to talk to whānau, hapū and iwi.

They gave us the details of their deal, and I said, 'I'm not taking that out to iwi. It's a perpetual-lease system.' I told them I much preferred partnerships, so we went back to them with the concept of creating a 50/50 joint venture with landowners.

My focus right from the start has really been aimed at Māori, because a lot of the lands Māori were left after colonial land grabs were called marginal lands, unsuited to agriculture. But they are very good for carbon sinks, which I believe will be increasingly important because of climate change.

Under New Zealand's climate change mitigation policy, any new forests planted after January 1990 are potentially eligible to receive carbon credits under the Emissions Trading Scheme, and so carbon farming is an opportunity for Māori landowners to receive carbon credits from reforestation or afforestation. Once the government started saying that it will lift the cap, it's become a lot safer for investors. So that's a bit of work in progress there. I've got a full programme sorted out.

I tell people that one of the poetic things about this whole proposal is that their lands were once described as the wastelands of New Zealand, and now they've got a big value, because they are prime lands for growing carbon. There will be a demand for them and they're going to get people knocking on their doors left, right and centre.

At a presentation in Hastings an old lady asked

me, 'Dear, what if someone comes and offers a better deal than you? Should I take it?'

'We deliberately set the figure at 50/50, because if someone wants to beat it, they've got to eat into their own profit to give you more. So if someone comes and offers you more, take it. It's money,' I said.

At a meeting in Kaitāia, a guy came and came and came at us with questions, and I answered everything. At the end, he stood up and said, 'Well, whānau, I'm a forester and this is the best deal in the country,' which of course is what we believe.

It is very good money for landowners, most of whom have no funding and have no income from their land. All they had to put up is time — that's the beauty of it.

Carbon trading is a simple little mechanism, and there's too many countries now involved in it for it to disappear.

The ultimate would be to use native trees, because over its lifetime, native forest of New Zealand will sequester about 42 times more carbon than *Pinus radiata*. But New Zealand native forest is such a slow grower that it's an intergenerational investment. Certainly, *Pinus radiata* is a much faster return. My heart tells me that the best thing for New Zealand is to plant natives, but if I want to do it purely for an economic return, it's not going to happen. We've told everyone that we will not plant exotics along rivers because that's where you have your natives to act as a buffer to keep your rivers clean. But, really, you can only do it at about a 30/70 mix. If you go above 30 per cent native, it becomes uneconomic because the natives are so slow growing.

It's a matter of getting through to people that when you're involved in carbon farming, it's a no-brainer with cashflow. Most iwi landowners have never had any capital off their properties, so this is a good way of bringing them into it. When you cut a pine forest, it creates a terrible mess. We hear a lot about that lately. But carbon farmers don't cut the trees and therefore don't have those risks, like the floods that carry all the stumpage and then choke the rivers and beaches with it.

We've held a lot of hui up north. We point out that these things take time when there are multiple owners and the Māori world works differently. And that the best thing is that the whenua, the land, stays with mana whenua. We absolutely can guarantee, no matter what happens to the forest, that they can't touch the land. It belongs to the owner.

Climate change

I'm often asked, 'What's the Māori view on global warming?'

'Well,' I reply, 'given that humans have never been through one, I'd say there's none. But there's a huge amount of mātauranga on adaptation.'

In a way, it's the reverse of the ice ages. When you have an ice age, there's a huge period of adaptation, the new growing cycles, the new temperatures, et cetera. That's what we'll go through with global warming, but when we get to a certain temperature what we're actually facing is mass extinction.

As a nation, Aotearoa is not making the changes we need to. Our emissions have risen. New Zealand has one of the highest rates of car ownership in the world. We're a small population, but we're also a major contributor based on our size. There's only a short window to act because the Kyoto Protocol only goes up to 2050. We don't know what will happen after that. I am so worried about this.

The big part with climate change is, well, change. People don't react well to change but we have to, because the planet is warming and we need to think about what sort of a world we are leaving for future generations. Change is often hard to contemplate, but it usually offers opportunity. What lessons can we take from the past? Well, all species have been through weather changes, and there is adaptability that comes from all those processes. We're just going to have to learn.

We're pretty dumb as a species. We think we can control nature to do what we want. Here in Canterbury, they drained the swamps and capped the springs. Well, that's all well and good, but those springs and rivers are still running underground. Then we had the earthquakes. Turns it into liquefaction. I remember sitting over at Rāpaki years ago when a Ngāi Tahu kaumātua, Bill Gillies, said, 'You wait. One day in the future, we'll have an earthquake, then they'll learn the folly of building on top of a swamp.'

That man was a prophet. We're arrogant to think we can manipulate the world.

What role do we have to play in adapting to climate change? Here's an example that affects the whole world, across all borders: to bring the stormwater infrastructure of New Zealand up to a level that can handle the new rain flows is going to cost around $230 billion. Who will pay for it?

Yet some still deny that climate change is occurring here. Do I think it's survivable? Yes, if we get our act together. When I say *we*, I mean the world's got to get its act together on this. We can all help. We will have no choice. We must. Those 2019–20 fires in Australia were definitely a wake-up call.

I notice our seasons are changing. An example this year was in the paddock in front of my house in Ōaro, where the kōwhai was in full flower at the end of July. That's about two and a half months ahead of time. And we've had a massive drop in the number of seabirds in Kaikōura. In 1999, Kaikōura had 23,000 roosting red-billed gulls, which was the fourth-biggest population in the country. We now have 11,000, the biggest population in the country. There is absolute evidence that the red-billed gull has reduced in size. They're a smaller bird than they were 50 years ago. That's food-related.

With the oceans heating up, there has been a temperature change in the Tasman Sea. There are waters off the Chatham Rise that are 6 degrees warmer than they used to be and that changes current flows. You can see from satellite pictures now that warm currents are heading south and this is what the fish are following. So all the food flows will change, the plankton supplies will change. The fish are moving south, which means that the traditional fishing grounds are going to change.

Snapper's now becoming a bit of a pest off Taranaki, where previously they used Taranaki as a highway to come down into southern waters. Normally, snapper come into our waters at the start of spring and towards the end of autumn they head back, because snapper like waters around 18 degrees. Well, they're not going back anymore; they're staying all year round. They were catching snapper off Greymouth in the middle of winter. They're catching snapper and kingfish in Foveaux Strait.

Everything's in flux. In a couple of decades, there's going to be a totally new fishery. We're going to have to find out where the new fishing grounds are, where the new spawning grounds are, and where the new food flows are to stay viable. From a Māori perspective, it's a billion-dollar industry for us, so this is critical.

Given that roughly 61 per cent of all Māori investment is in primary industries, climate change will have a dramatic effect on us economically. Whatever's coming, we're locked into it. Even if the world made the decision to ban all carbon, it would still take the planet about 400 to 500 years to recognise it, and then around 1000 to 2000 years to reverse it.

The last Intergovernmental Panel on Climate Change (IPCC) report basically gave us 14 years to make changes. If global temperatures rise more than 1.5 degrees Celsius, then we face the risk of rising seas, increasing heatwaves and a very different world to the one we live in now. Sadly, there is no world leadership and no acknowledgement of the lessons of the past.

I was in Southland a few years ago when the big boom was starting in dairy, and an elder told me how most of Southland in the 1950s was dairy but then they had three wet winters in a row. The Southland top soils are quite thin and so after those three winters, when they went into a dry spell, the weight of the cattle basically turned all the paddocks into concrete. They had to resow all the paddocks and everyone reverted back to sheep. Now they're doing the whole thing again in pursuit of short-term gain, with no recognition of the lessons of the past.

Look at the latest data on the Amazon rainforest, which indicates that by 2050 it'll start releasing carbon. The rainforest will no longer be a carbon sink. It will be a carbon emitter. All these things are signs of climate change. It worries me.

I accepted the invitation to go on the governance group of the Deep South National Science Challenge after a conversation with Trevor Burt, who was then the chair of Ngāi Tahu Holdings. I wanted to know what risk analysis around climate change had been carried out before what is now Ngāi Tahu Farms converted forestry to farmland in North Canterbury. They came back four days later and said that because Ngāi Tahu owned 30,000 acres of forest on the West Coast, it was carbon neutral. That's good, I said, but that wasn't my question.

I wanted to know about risk analysis because all indications are that Canterbury, North Canterbury and Marlborough are heading into a long-term drought. It didn't make sense to be investing up to $700 million in water-intensive farming, let alone investigate the question of ownership. They had converted Eyrewell, a large forest Ngāi Tahu owns in North Canterbury, into dairy farms before the data was really on the table. But they acknowledged that water-intensive farming wasn't sustainable in the long run, pulled the plug on converting Balmoral, which is also an uneconomic forest in North Canterbury, and were investigating crops and trees that were sustainable.

Māori are used to living sustainably and have proved to be innovative in the face of challenges, so I think we are well placed.

Ko ngā hau ki ētahi wāhi,
ko ngā kai ki Orariki.

Whatever the season or wind,
food will be found at Orariki.

Abuse

One of the biggest issues around colonisation is that when Europeans came to New Zealand, under law their women and children were chattels, owned by their fathers or their husbands. In Māori society, there were no gender roles. A Māori woman could be a war leader, a community leader, a tohunga.

One of the first things the missionaries did was try to break down the agency of Māori women, because Pākehā women had none. The missionaries brought with them the concepts of 'spare the rod, spoil the child', and that children are to be seen and not heard. That was absolutely contrary to te ao Māori. My argument is that we have got to get back to where we were, when a woman had a role equal with men, and children belonged to the community. In that time, when a woman married into another iwi and was abused, that didn't just become an issue for her whānau, that became a hapū issue, because the abuse was hurting whakapapa. Our people took abuse seriously then, and it could lead to war.

Several years ago, there was a major issue about historic abuse in Kaikōura that I got involved in when a cousin rang me up with some information and that led to a list of names and some big allegations. We called a hui at Takahanga Marae. Twenty-three people turned up and 12 women and two men stood up and talked about their experiences of being raped.

We called sexual abuse counsellors in and some of the women got strong. They stepped up and made complaints even though they faced being vilified. This issue split our community between support for the victims and support for the alleged perpetrators. The damage is worst for those who want this to stay hidden. They don't want anyone to talk about it.

We all have a duty to talk about this. We know domestic violence, and that includes sexual abuse, goes on, but for far too long it has been ignored or brushed under the carpet. We all know this is going on in our families, but we never challenge the abusers. We need to have a conversation. It needs to be something we can openly talk about.

At Te Pūtahitanga, we have navigators whose sole role is working on family violence and sexual abuse. I started a programme called Tū Pono: Te Mana Kaha o te Whānau, which is a whānau-driven movement to find a way forward for Māori to prevent family violence. I spoke at a number of hui in Te Waipounamu and called on everyone to speak about this in public. I believe it is up to whānau to take a lead in bringing about change.

I'm on Interim Te Rōpū, a Māori advisory group to the government's joint venture to look at a strategy for dealing with family violence and sexual abuse. I'm also on another committee that is looking at an independent complaints process and monitoring. Complaints will go through the Ombudsman's office and the Children's Commissioner's role will be beefed up to take on two roles.

The other part of it will be to monitor the performance of Oranga Tamariki Ministry for Children. In the first quarter of 2019, there were 154 cases of abuse affecting 103 tamariki in care. Six of the abusers were Oranga Tamariki staff while 33 per cent were abused by extended whānau. And prior to the agreement to hold the Royal Commission of Inquiry into Abuse in Care, there were well over 1000 claims already on the table.

When I was brought in to have a look at their processes, I said, 'You got to be kidding me. This is how it works, isn't it? I'm a child that's been taken into care. While I'm in care, I'm physically and sexually abused. Then a period comes where you can make a claim, but I have to make the claim to the same people who took me and put me into those circumstances, and you will adjudicate whether my claim can be heard or not. Don't you think that's a conflict of interest?'

To be blunt, it's a bit like the Treaty of Waitangi settlements. The thief makes a determination on the compensation, whether you accept it or not; it still leaves a bloody dubious taste in your mouth because you know the process is not just. This is what is being advocated. It is perpetuating violence again.

When they sent me out to interview some of the claimants, I interviewed a 56-year-old woman. When she was seven, she and her six siblings had been put into care because of their mum's mental-health issues. Forty-nine years later, she had found one of her siblings. She cannot find the rest because everything about her family is redacted in her documentation.

I interviewed a group of men and heard things like, 'Oh, I got my application in five years ago and I got a letter saying it had been received but that's all I've heard in five years.' Another one hadn't heard anything in 18 months.

The Family Court process is not working. When I met with nine Family Court judges, I said, 'With all due respect, your process has destroyed this family, whose only crime was to have a mum who was sick. You've become so risk-averse that if my daughter got into trouble with her child, as a grandparent I've got absolutely no rights. I can't even attend the family group conference because I've got a conflict of interest, but they're part of my family.'

But it's not everything like you hear on TV. Of the 4600 Māori children currently held in care, 80 per cent are with the extended family. The issue is around the 20 per cent of children who have been swallowed up by the state. Part of the problem is that Oranga Tamariki goes straight to the court and cuts out process. The other part is they've become punitive. An example: there's a Māori NGO who had contracted 23 caregivers, all of whom were looking after children through Oranga Tamariki. Some of them had multiple children. When there was an alleged complaint against one of them, Oranga Tamariki's response was to remove the children from all 23. Five months later, Oranga Tamariki comes back, 'Ah, excuse me, there was no complaint after all. Can you take the children back?' They had already disrupted them, and now they wanted to disrupt them again. The answer was no.

But my biggest gripe with Oranga Tamariki is over this 'first thousand days' issue. All children naturally bond to a single individual in their first thousand days and it's usually Mum. You can remove the child from Mum and put him or her with another woman or a man and they will still bond. But if you break it again, they won't. Now you take a scan of a child that's been through the bond and when you look at a scan of the brain, the whole front is red — it's lit up.

In comparison, the brain scan of a child who's been raised without that parental bond shows that half of the frontal lobe is black, and it's the emotional side. So that's the kid who will just rush out onto the road without thinking. That's the kid who'll blow his fuse or the kid who can't concentrate. They've lost emotional control, and 92 per cent of those kids who have the bond broken will end up in jail. Now Oranga Tamariki, the Crown and all of these organisations have known about these studies for over 20 years but still they continually break the bond by moving the child from person to person. You could excuse it if they didn't know, but they do.

One of the key things identified about kids held in care and reported to the Royal Commission was that they felt stigmatised. They felt singled out. Of course they do. Why am I here? I didn't do anything wrong; it was Mum or it was Dad, they are thinking. All the major Māori gang members started as kids held in care. They were taught the violence while in care.

If you look at the breakdown of the evidence within the Family Court, as an example, a Māori woman going into the Family Court situation seeking a protection order is four to six times more likely to have her child taken from her and that child put into the control of the perpetrator of the violence.

I said in front of the Family Court judges, 'Any sane person has got to ask the question, "Why would you do that?" Why would you put the children with the perpetrator of the violence? It's almost like you're blaming the mother for being a victim of family violence from those men.'

There are five areas in the north where Māori women are between 62 per cent and 69 per cent of all the victims of family violence. You look at that evidence on its own and think, what's going on here? But a breakdown of the perpetrators of that violence shows it was actually equal: 50 per cent Pākehā and 50 per cent Māori men. In my head, that immediately says: This isn't a race issue. It's a male issue.

But the whole approach of government seems to be one of looking for deficits. Take all the deaths of Māori kids. Do you realise it actually makes up 0.009 per cent of the population? The death of any child is terrible but put it into perspective: 69 deaths in 10 years in over 758,000 people. Again, put it into perspective: 98 per cent of all Māori children have a brilliant upbringing and loving families. There's an issue around the rest.

When I spoke at the Ngāi Tahu Hui-ā-Tau, the tribe's annual meeting, in 2015 in Dunedin, I began my speech with some of the family violence statistics on the screen behind me.

'This is us,' I said, when I had finished listing them. 'We're all part of these statistics. And the reason it continues is because we keep turning our backs. "It's not my family, it's the one across the road," we say. Well, it is in your family,' I said. 'What are you doing about it?

'People say that the foundation of Māori culture is whakapapa. Well, any woman, child or man who's being abused is part of that whakapapa. So how come we keep turning our heads away and saying it's not happening. We must stop turning away and start challenging family violence because it is not acceptable.'

Māori women make up roughly 7 per cent of the population, but they're close to being 50 per cent of all victims of family violence. How does that happen?

I was in a meeting with Andrew Becroft, the Children's Commissioner, and a comment was made about a case in Flaxmere, Hawke's Bay, where the whole whānau had closed ranks and were supposedly refusing to talk to the police. The first time I ever heard of that happening was in the case of the Kahui twins, who died in hospital in 2006 with serious head injuries. The second time I heard about a case like that was Nia Glassie. She was the three-year-old whose death sparked national outrage. This case of a young boy in Flaxmere was the third time I'd heard of a whānau refusing to talk to the cops.

Judge Becroft also only knew of those three cases. So why all the rhetoric about 'Māori, get your shit together', I wanted to know, when there were so few cases to quote. Three families out of how many? Māori always get picked on and highlighted for the number of children who have been killed over the past 30 years, yet our 18 per cent of deaths is far less than 82 per cent of Pākehā children.

'Oh, no,' someone at the meeting said. 'It's because on a per capita basis, Māori are the highest.' Yes, but how many of those Māori children were killed by their Pākehā parent, I wanted to know. Because quite a few were. If you take that out, we weren't the highest. But it seems as though there is always finger pointing and lumping Māori together as one.

All Māori kids hear about their people, out of the mouths of politicians and the media, is negative, negative, negative. The reality is that 98 per cent of Māori children are brought up in loving, caring homes. Yes, there's an issue around a small percentage, but a good part of that issue is the racism that comes from Pākehā.

And now some Māori want to get rid of Oranga Tamariki. Well, hang on, all this is based on a TV programme about the uplift of a child in Hawke's Bay. Where were you when the other 4600 were taken? Because you were absolutely silent. You do not throw out the whole structure over an issue of 20 per cent. You fix the bloody issue.

As the internal review of the Oranga Tamariki uplift at Hawke's Bay shows, Oranga Tamariki had shortcut the process by going straight to the uplift. They're not, by their own Act, allowed to do that unless a child has been killed and if they have a specific court order. Other than that, they have absolutely no legal right to uplift, but they've been doing it non-stop. It's an attitudinal thing.

If you look at the data, Māori violence against children has dramatically dropped since 2013, but uplifts have dramatically increased, and the number of unnotified uplifts has dramatically increased also. How come? The data doesn't stack up.

Data again is interesting when you look at it on a per capita basis. Māori make up 15 per cent of the population, but the figures look a lot higher from a per capita perspective than Pākehā. The bureaucrats in Wellington put up a draft of their plan to stop family violence. It had sections on Māori violence, Pasifika violence, Asian and ethnic violence, violence against the elderly and violence against those with disabilities, who are the most heavily offended against in the world.

I asked, 'Where's the Pākehā violence?'

'Oh, it's not as bad,' they said.

I gave a speech in 2018 in Ōtautahi at the Museums Aotearoa conference. They had given me a theme: 'Do museums have a responsibility to raise social consciousness?' I titled my speech 'A Walk on the Dark Side of New Zealand'. Afterwards, 20 minutes were allocated for questions. A woman in the front row of the Isaac Theatre Royal stood up. 'Can I please ask: if anyone in this audience has been a victim of either family violence or sexual abuse, would you please stand?'

Over 60 per cent of the audience got to their feet. All Pākehā. Just in this city, Ōtautahi, there are roughly 2500 police call-outs to violence and abuse cases a month. Of those, 1500 are Pākehā families, 600 are Māori families, 300 Pasifika, 100 Asian. It doesn't matter which police district you go into; they can put up a series of maps of their district showing every house that they go to on a regular basis.

Our approach to family violence is wrong. Everything we do is about the ambulance at the bottom of the cliff. What we don't do enough of is primary intervention, which is better education. My view is that the only people who can stop family violence, given that 90 per cent of all sexual abuse is either within the family or with close family friends, is whānau. We've got to confront what's in front of us, which is what I did at home in Kaikōura. It doesn't always make you popular.

Water

When we were kids, we could dive off the railway bridge into our river at Ōaro, it was that deep. Do that now and you're dead, because the awa doesn't have the flow that it used to have.

Iwi and Māori have a role to play in ensuring that our water is looked after for future generations, and that it is not seen solely as a resource to be exploited. The concept of Te Mana o te Wai, which simply means that the first right belongs to the river, is now part of legislation. Under this concept, the mauri and the mana of the wai belongs to that body of water. We all have a responsibility to protect, nurture and care for the wai.

And under that first right is the guarantee of

a minimum-flow regime that protects the whole ecology of the river system. Once you've done that, then humans can have a look at the take. But unless you guarantee that minimum-flow regime, you destroy the river and you destroy the ecology that goes with it.

I was, for a period, the co-chair of the Freshwater Iwi Leaders Group, which was set up in 2005. The first meeting was called by Tā Tumu Te Heuheu and he invited Waikato Tainui, Te Arawa, Whanganui and Ngāi Tahu to the meeting because collectively we have the biggest water bodies within our respective takiwā.

The biggest issue confronting Aotearoa over water is the grandfather clause, which holds that the first in is the first served. Most rights to take water are under the old water systems, like the canals, which are the most inefficient way of transporting water for irrigation. Up to 30 per cent of that water just evaporates off. And because they've got that first right, it's a perpetual right. They might have to renew it every 35 years, but it's automatically granted to them.

The other thing that is interesting is that very few iwi or hapū in the country support the concept of trading rights for water. We have drawn attention to the quota management system for the fisheries. Thirty years after the introduction of that system for commercial fishing, 80 per cent of all the deep-water quotas of this country are owned by three companies. If you had a tradeable system for water, you'd end up with a similar situation.

I have no issue with a farmer trading their water to another farmer along the catchment. Take the Waiau-uha, also known as the Waiau River, which has the second-largest catchment of North Canterbury's rivers: when they decided on regulations, they based them on a water meter that was at the top end of the river, but the one down the bottom had been broken for over 15 years. While it showed a good flow regime at the top end of the river, it was a totally different story down the bottom.

So, at times on the Waiau, the farmers inland up the top end get plenty of water, but the farmers down the bottom get hardly anything. What we were saying is, in that instance, the farmer at the top can trade some water with the farmer down the bottom, but if you apply for a consent to irrigate your land, that should be the only thing you're allowed to do with it.

If you're not going to use it for your land, then put

it back in the river, so the next person can have a bite of the cherry. I do absolutely believe that iwi have a right to a reasonable share of water. You can't have mahinga kai, food gathering, without water. It is as simple as that.

This is not about ownership of water, but rather it's more that iwi have right of access to water in their tribal takiwā. Take Ngāti Kurī, my people, for example: our southern boundary is the Hurunui River. Do we want more of the Hurunui? Of course we do. We've got 6500 hectares there, tribally. The next river along is the Waiau. We've got 9500 hectares there, and of course we want water. But the next main river is the Conway. Neither the tribe nor any hapū has any lands along the Conway River. Why would we want water access? I'd certainly want to use my kaitiaki role and be able to have an input into the minimum-flow regimes for the Hurunui and Waiau.

But to me this is not about owning water; it's about how we treat it. There are plenty of things we can do to minimise our use of water, but we're not good at it. We still have the dumb farmers out there who have their irrigators on in a full northwest wind in Canterbury, or council parks with the irrigators on during a northwester.

Regenerative farming absolutely reduces the amount of water needed. To me, regenerative farming is a bit like going back to the old days, where your let your lands go fallow. You rotate your crops because if you put the same crop in each year, it leaches the land, but if you have different crops, it's much kinder on the land.

Everything we do, we can improve on. New Zealanders have been very wasteful in their use of water. We all know that. The attitudes of Cantabrians to water compared to Aucklanders who have to pay for everything, including their wastewater, is totally different.

Racism

My neighbour is a retired police officer. I was talking to him about what it was like on his first day on the force and he told me that his sergeant said, 'Just because you see a Māori driving a car at three in the morning does not mean they're a burglar, but there's probably a 98 per cent chance they are.' There's a whole police force that has been brought up thinking like that.

Our problem here is not so much the violence of police against Māori, it's the overcharging. Māori are four to six times more likely to be stopped by a police officer. They are six times more likely to be charged. They are four times more likely to be multiply charged. Even when they get into the court system, they are

11.5 times more likely to be remanded in custody. And based on the latest data that's come out, Māori are seven and a half times more likely to be jailed.

I said to the statistician for the Ministry of Justice that it only tells you a small part of the story of the person. And I said to him, 'Well, if Māori — and this is your department's data — are eleven and a half times more likely to be remanded in custody and seven and a half times more likely to be jailed, that bias must have a huge economic cost. Does that mean Māori justice is more expensive?'

At the first meeting of Interim Te Rōpū, which is trying to develop a national strategy about domestic violence, the chief executive of the joint venture business unit, the Crown agency, said to me, 'Do you realise there are nearly 4000 Māori in gangs?'

I said, 'I do know that. Do you know that they make up 0.4 per cent of the Māori population, which tells me that 99.6 per cent of Māori are not in gangs? Have you considered looking at it like that?'

'Oh, well,' she said. 'You can't deny the prison populations are mainly Māori.'

'I don't deny it,' I said, 'but when there is a system where Māori are four to six times more likely to be charged, then simple mathematics would tell you that the biggest populations in the prisons have a brown skin.'

When Paula Bennett was the Minister of Youth Affairs, she was a keynote speaker at an Iwi Leaders Forum. She stepped up to the podium, looked at the audience, and she saw me. 'Oh, Ngāi Tahu,' she said, 'You have 80 children under state care. Ngāpuhi, you're the worst in the country. You've got 389.' And she named all the tribes and finished with this comment: 'It is time you people took recognition of this issue and helped pay for it.'

The following Monday, I was in her office.

'Minister,' I said, 'I've come to talk to you about your speech. Please don't think I'm trying to minimise the issue, because one child in state care is one too many in my opinion. But my issue was your messaging. You point to me in a public forum and say, "Ngāi Tahu, you have 80 children under state care." What you didn't add to that data is, "Ngāi Tahu, you have 64,000 members on your tribal registry." If you do the maths, minister, 80 children is just over 0.1 per cent of our population. You make a very loud and cruel statement about Ngāpuhi being the worst in the country at 389, but with all due respect, they have in excess of 127,000 members, so the so-called worst in the country is less than 0.4 per cent of the population.

'As a nation, too often we focus on deficit thinking; it's no wonder that people look at Māori kids and go, "My god, they're going off the rails." Well, why don't you try a different message? Why don't you try a bit of positive reinforcement, instead of the constant negatives about us?'

To her credit, she apologised and said she hadn't thought of it like that.

All the racism that surfaced around the mosque shootings in Ōtautahi wasn't new. That's been going on for years in this country. I was amazed at the Justice hui in 2019, when the Māori lawyer Moana Jackson gave the fourth update to a report that he first put out in 1988, which was really about racism in this country. He opened with the comment that he was deeply saddened to say the only difference today from his original report was that Māori women's incarceration rates had gone up by 25 per cent. Other than that, it was exactly the same as it was in 1988.

Despite that, I'm optimistic about change. I think things are changing in Aotearoa, because race relations here are being talked about more, and the Black Lives Matter movement overseas is certainly helping. Since 2007, the heads of the police have actively been trying to remove the bias within the system. There is racism in the police and it's going to take a generation to weed it out, but the police are trying from the top to remove that bias.

If you look at the narrative that comes through the media, it stems from the politicians; everything about the Māori world is doom and gloom. But when you go into the communities, it's not like that. Yes, there are issues, and everybody knows there are issues, but also everyone's striving to go forward. But all we seem to get fed to us is the negative side.

We have known for decades that there's a whole different regime of charging Māori and Pasifika for crimes. We've known for decades that there are more Māori sentences in court. And it still continues. All of this has been public for decades, and we're still doing it.

I love data. Data can be skewed, but also you can really illustrate things with it and stop a lot of shit.

Here's an example. There are 83,500 young Māori not in education, work or training. But when it comes to the funding that's allocated to those types of issues, Māori get 2 per cent. It's crazy.

In 2020, I was sitting on a plane beside the head of the road police. 'You know what cracks me up?' I said as we chatted. 'That 23 per cent of male Māori in jail are in for traffic-related offences. And the data clearly shows that for up to 88 per cent of all prisoners, regardless of their race, who are in jail and are male, their first offence or first brush with the law is either because they have been driving without a licence, driving without a warrant or driving without a registration.

'If we would only get our heads out of our arses and introduce driving as part of the school curriculum, for $850 we could get them a full licence and put them through a defensive driving course. But we don't bother to do that. Instead, we'd rather jail them at $95,000 a year. This is absolutely ridiculous.'

He agreed, and said they'd been arguing that for 20 years. So, why, I wanted to know, were the two highest areas for traffic fines in Canterbury — Aranui and Hornby — also the two poorest suburbs? There are $1 million in fines every six months for two areas and those are the two places where people are the least likely to be able to pay fines. I didn't get an answer.

Again, it doesn't make any sense. At the moment, there is no justice, because there's such bias in the processes. Those figures around Māori being charged might shock some people but that's the way it has been for decades. First the Crown waited for Māori to die out, and then successive governments tried to assimilate Māori and turn us into Pākehā. Now it is changing; rangatahi think it is cool to be Māori. There will be even more change as our demographics change and there are more young Māori, but there is an urgent need to change the bias in the system.

Faith

Religion has been a big part of my life. Mum and Dad had me christened and I had my first communion in Ōaro, but it was my decision to attend church. I used to get up every Sunday and go to church because I liked the structure. I like the beliefs, if they are adhered to properly, and all of the teachings of the Bible. It's about respect for your fellow person. I've always been comfortable in the Catholic faith. I became an altar boy because I liked it. I liked the process, the ceremony. I've always believed that there is a creator and if there is a classic creation, then we're all part of it.

Still, there's lots of things the Catholic church does that I'm absolutely ashamed of, right up to the Pope, who's hidden all this stuff, or tried to brush it under the carpet. It's shameful. But it doesn't mean that the religion is wrong. It's the people who are involved that are in the wrong. I see religion as a recipe, a blueprint for how we should live as community. But we're not good at actually following what our religions teach. The true meaning of Catholicism is community and sharing prayer together. The teachings are quite beautiful.

I walked away from the church for a while when my dad died because I blamed God. But I got over that sulk after a few years. All my kids are christened and baptised and had their first Holy Communion and all that stuff, and from then on it's their business. They tell me they hated it but I forced them to go through it. Well, one day it'll become important to them. No one's an atheist when they're facing danger, I say.

We're also part of nature yet we seem to think that we rule nature. We don't. The Māori way is very practical. Take the story of Poutini, which is a widely known Ngāi Tahu story. Poutini is a taniwha who falls in love with Waitaiki, near the island of Tūhua, also known as Mayor Island in the Bay of Plenty, and steals her away to Te Waipounamu, pursued by her husband, the chief known as Tamaahua.

You could look at it as a lovely myth of a taniwha

or sea monster that steals a woman, Waitaiki, but actually another way of looking at it is as a geological map of New Zealand in waiata or song form, because Māori had an oral culture and waiata was one way of remembering and passing on information. Every place that Tamaahua chases Poutini to as he tries to get his wife back is a place where pre-European Māori got different types of stone for weapons and tools. It is why Hokitika on the West Coast is known as pounamu or jade country. To Māori, the West Coast of the South Island is known as Te Tai o Poutini or simply Tai Poutini.

Each time Poutini stopped, he lit a fire to warm Waitaiki: at Tahanga, on the Coromandel Peninsula at Whangamatā, in Taupō, at Rangitoto ki te Tonga D'Urville Island, Onetahua, otherwise known as Farewell Spit, and Pahuatare on the West Coast. The rocks at all these sites were important sources of stone for Māori. Eventually, Poutini realised that Tamaahua will never stop his pursuit and turned Waitaiki into his essence, into pounamu.

Fundamentalism is a problem in whichever religion you find it. I'll use this as an example:

I was invited to attend Destiny Church's launch of its political party, or what I thought was the launch of a political party. It turned out to be the day Brian Tamaki apologised to the gay community. There were over 2000 people there on a Saturday morning and that stunned me. I thought I'd go back the next day for the service and see what the numbers were like. Well, it was packed.

Hannah Tamaki, Brian's wife, opened the service. She saw me in the audience and invited me to come up. So I got up, and I said, 'Bishop Brian, I was here yesterday and I heard your apology to the gay community and I felt that it was genuine. But you have to acknowledge, you do say some silly things, like when you blamed the earthquakes in Christchurch on the gay community. Now, you know, I do believe that faith can move mountains, but I didn't know it could move tectonic plates. And if it can, and the gay community can do this, then I better get off this waka.'

Then I picked up his Bible and said, 'I've read this from cover to cover. Nowhere in here, in the New Testament, does it talk about hate and intolerance. But your comments promote hate and intolerance. You can't call yourself a Christian if you're going to talk like that.'

A final word

I don't think I am feisty but I think I've got a decent moral code. And if people are doing things that I think are incorrect, I will stand up and challenge them. I've always been against bullies and I'll always stand up for people.

On the day I was appointed to Te Rūnanga o Ngāi Tahu, I asked one of our kaumātua, 'Why did you nominate me?'

And he said, 'We accept that you're from a chiefly line. But you're the only one that will challenge if you think things are being done wrong. We trust you to look after our interests.'

I was lucky to witness a period when Ngāi Tahu were able to provide enormous opportunities for its rangatahi, thanks to the settlement, and thanks to our settlement team, known as the A-team, and mainly to Tā Tipene O'Regan, who was definitely the man for a very complex job. And it was also thanks to people like Sid Ashton, a Pākehā who was the first chief executive of Te Rūnanga o Ngāi Tahu and the man many credit for our early success.

It is known within the tribe, although perhaps not so well known elsewhere, that in 1849 our Ngāi Tahu tipuna Matiaha Tiramōrehu sent Queen Victoria a petition signed by all the leading Ngāi Tahu chiefs of the time asking for justice, after Ngāi Tahu had sold 34.5 million acres of land to the Crown and didn't receive either the promised price or the 10 per cent of land promised as reserves.

Over the next seven generations, many people contributed to what was known as Te Kerēme — the Ngāi Tahu Claim. We are known both within the tribe and outside of Ngāi Tahu as the people of the long memory. We don't forget. We were sure we would get some kind of justice, and we did. It wasn't anywhere near what we lost over that period of time, but the settlement allowed us to move forward.

There's no doubt our settlement created huge opportunities for our people. There's no doubt in my mind that Ngāi Tahu is more embedded in society than the tribe was before. Just look at what has been achieved in Ōtautahi since the earthquakes and at the presence we now have in the city. Our rangatahi now have huge opportunities in employment and education, to name just two sectors, because of the settlement. Up until 1998, we only had the Ngāi Tahu Māori Trust Board to represent us. It did a marvellous job, but settlement enabled the tribe to move forward into opportunities for our people in a way that had not been possible previously.

Māori have an important role to play in this country and our country's collective outlook is definitely changing. It is cool to be Māori these days. The early settlers tried to wipe out Māori; when that didn't work, the goal was to assimilate us, and that didn't work either. Now there is a renewed pride in being Māori. To be Māori these days and to know your culture, your language and your whakapapa gives you mana. I know who I am and where I came from; it engenders pride and it is a step forward from the intergenerational hardships our tīpuna had to deal with. There are definitely more opportunities for our rangatahi now.

Even though I am what I would describe as an iwi fundamentalist, a common misconception of the Māori economy is that it is driven by iwi or tribes, when a lot of it comes from whānau and hapū. There have been various estimates of the Māori economy but it is generally thought to be worth $68 billion, and growing faster than the overall economy of Aotearoa. This gives Māori an advantage they didn't have previously, but the overall benefit of being Māori is more than a simple economic equation; it's in our sense of connection, with each other and with nature and our long-term view.

The part Māori will play in the future of this country will depend on values and good leadership. In my eyes, good leadership is simple. It is about being honest and authentic, and valuing and listening to people. Those are the values I learnt early on, and I have tried to stay true to them throughout my life.

Glossary

ahi kā title to land through occupation, generally over a long period of time
āhua nature, character, way of being
ariki paramount chief
awa river
hapū subtribe
harirū part of the greeting process (coming from the English 'How do you do?')
hongi to press noses in greeting
hui meeting
iwi tribe
kai food
kaitiaki guardian, custodian
kaitiakitanga guardianship
kaiwhakahaere chair, director
kākahu ceremonial cloak
karanga to call, generally onto a marae
kaumātua elderly man or woman, a person of status
kaupapa purpose, method, programme, subject
kawa custom or protocol, usually in relation to marae
kete basket or bag
kōrero to speak, a discussion
kotahitanga unity, togetherness
mahau porch
mahinga kai garden or cultivation, a place where food is gathered

mana honour, prestige, status
manaaki to care for, support, protect
manaakitanga kindness, generosity, support
mana whenua territorial rights from tribal lands
manuhiri guests, visitors
marae incorporating the wharenui, a meeting place where formal greetings and discussions take place
mātāmua first-born child
matua father, uncle; often used for any senior male figure
mauri life force, vital essence
mihi thanks, acknowledgement, tribute
mokopuna grandchild or grandchildren; abbreviated to **moko**
pā fort or fortified village
paepae orators' bench on a marae
papatipu rūnanga regional councils of Ngāi Tahu
pou post, pillar
pounamu greenstone
pōwhiri welcome ceremony, to be welcomed
rangatahi younger generation, youth
rangatira chiefly leader
rangatiratanga chieftainship, chiefly autonomy; also sovereignty or self-determination
rohe boundaries or region, usually of an iwi
rōpū group
rūnanga tribal council, iwi authority
takiwā district, area
tangata whenua indigenous people, people of the land
tangi burial rites, funeral
taniwha water spirit or creature

tapu sacred, prohibited, protected
tāua elderly person
tautoko to support or advocate
te ao Māori the Māori world or worldview
tipuna ancestor; plural form is **tīpuna**
tohungatanga expertise, proficiency
tono to ask or request
tūtae excrement, shit
tūturu true, real, authentic
upoko customary head
urupā burial ground
waiata traditional song
waka boat or canoe; can also be used for other vehicles
whaikōrero formal oratory or speech-making
whakapapa ancestral line, descent, genealogy
whakataukī proverb or proverbial saying
whānau family or family group
whanaungatanga kinship, family connection, bond
whāngai a customary practice in which a child is raised by someone other than his or her birth parents, though they are often part of the whānau
whare house or building
wharenui meeting house on a marae
whenua land

Acknowledgements

To thank everyone by name would take an eternity, but I owe a huge debt to my wife Maria and my children. I couldn't have been kaiwhakahaere of Ngāi Tahu without the support of my wife, who was willing to put up with the hours I spent in service to the tribe. The support of my wife and family has been enormous.

Of course, I owe a big debt to my mum and dad, which should go without saying but I feel it is important to acknowledge.

I owe a huge debt to the seven generations of Ngāi Tahu who fought to right the injustice delivered to the tribe by the Crown. I wish to acknowledge the members of Ngāi Tahu who passed knowledge and traditions down through those generations and helped deliver a bright future for the tribe.

I also want to thank Mark Revington for his unstinting work in helping me put this book together. And thanks to Nicola Legat of Massey University Press for commissioning the book.

Mark Solomon

About the authors

Tā Mark Wiremu Solomon KNZM, Ngāi Tahu, Ngāti Kurī, served as kaiwhakahaere of Te Rūnanga o Ngāi Tahu, the tribal council of Ngāi Tahu, for approximately 18 years, from 1998 until 2016. He was founder of the Iwi Chairs Forum, and stepped down as deputy chair of the Canterbury District Health Board in late 2020.

Mark Revington is a freelance journalist who has worked for many leading publications including the *National Business Review*, the *New Zealand Listener* and *Unlimited*. His awards include Westpac Financial Journalist of the Year and Business Magazine Editor of the Year. He spent six or so years working for Te Rūnanga o Ngāi Tahu.

Index

Page numbers in **bold** indicate images

MASSEY UNIVERSITY PRESS

First published in 2021 by Massey University Press
Private Bag 102904, North Shore Mail Centre
Auckland 0745, New Zealand
www.masseypress.ac.nz

Design by Megan van Staden
Cover photograph by Tony Bridge

A catalogue record for this book is available from the National Library of New Zealand

Printed and bound in China by Everbest Investment Ltd

ISBN: 978-0-9951354-3-7
eISBN: 978-0-9951465-4-9